You Didn't Hear It from Us

You Didn't Hear It from Us

Two Bartenders Serve Women the Truth About Men, Making an Impression, and Getting What You Want

DUSHAN ZARIC & JASON KOSMAS

ATRIA BOOKS

New York   London   Toronto   Sydney

ATRIA BOOKS

1230 Avenue of the Americas
New York, NY 10020

Library of Congress Cataloging-in-Publication Data

Zaric, Dushan.
    You didn't hear it from us : two bartenders serve women the truth about men,
making an impression, and getting what you want / Dushan Zaric & Jason Kosmas.
-- 1st Atria Books hardcover ed.
        p. cm.
    1. Man-woman relationships.   2. Women—Psychology.   3. Men—Psychology.
4. Dating (Social customs).   I. Kosmas, Jason.   II. Title.

HQ801.Z37 2006
646.7'7—dc22   2006047647

ISBN-13: 978-0-7432-9343-3
ISBN-10:   0-7432-9343-6

First Atria Books hardcover edition November 2006

1   3   5   7   9   10   8   6   4   2

ATRIA BOOKS is a trademark of Simon & Schuster, Inc.

Manufactured in the United States of America

Design by Dana Sloan

For information about special discounts for bulk purchases,
please contact Simon & Schuster Special Sales at
1-800-456-6798 or business @ simonandschuster.com.

Contents

Introduction

We can't get you laid. We can't find you your husband. But we can show you how to do it all by yourself. When it comes to guys, you think it's a game. You think it's a mystery. Well, sure—if you don't know the secrets. But you're in luck, because we do. And we're going to give them to you. Who are we? Why do we have all the answers? We're your bartenders. We're the guys who watch you, every single night. You put on your best clothes, your best smile, and once again, you strike out. Sometimes you cry. Sometimes you just slink off. But either way, the end result is the same: You assume there must be something wrong with *you*. You're too fat. You're not charming. You aren't clever, you don't know how to flirt. And it all boils down to one simple fact of which you've convinced yourself: No one will ever want you.

You couldn't be more wrong. Because all these men are looking for you, as hard as you're looking for them. But when you think you're showing off your pretty skirt, you're missing that that's *all* you're showing off. Because you've left the *real* you at home. That warm, funny person you really are is sitting on the couch drowning her sorrows in a gallon of Ben and Jerry's and watching *Desperate Housewives* reruns, while your alter ego has taken your cutest outfit out to the bar and isn't doing it much good. Men don't care that much about your cute skirt. But men *really* care about what's under it. (And yes, for the moment, we mean your personality.)

Between the two of us, we've spent approximately thirty years in a bar. We've watched every hookup imaginable. We've seen every embarrassing fuckup. We know who is going to send a drink before they even think of it; we know that handsome guy you're trying to get up the nerve to talk to is gay. We know that while you're talking about Iraq you're busy obsessing that your short dress is showing your imagined cellulite. We see you trying to impress men who only want to watch the basketball game playing behind you, while you ignore the great, receptive guy standing right next to you. We watch it *every* single night.

If you only knew all of this, you'd be set. But you're not going to hear the truth from your father or your brother. And you're certainly not going to hear it from your best friend. You might not like some of the things we're going to say, but hear us out anyway. Because, for better or worse, you want to be successful with men. You want to be one of those women you've always watched who seems to get every guy. And that's the first secret. To be *with* men, you gotta get 'em first. As in, understand who they are. And then, understand what they want, what turns them on, and what turns them off.

But in order to do that, in order to learn how to seduce a man, you need to do something far more difficult than getting a man into bed. You have to learn about yourself. You have to learn to accept yourself, and then how to show off those things in you that make you such a strong, vibrant person.

There's not a soul on this planet who doesn't have something wonderful to offer. The trick is to first really look inward and find your strengths. And next to recognize what you see as your weaknesses. In doing this, you can accept who you are, and then do the most important thing you will ever do in your life: Take responsibility for yourself. Take responsibility for the part you play in the dramas that unfold. Once you do that, you can change the story. *Your* story.

And what you'll find, in the process of doing this, is that you are suddenly attracting more men than you ever have before, even while you weren't necessarily trying. It can be a long process, but the good news is that as you begin the journey, you *can* fake it till you make it. You can, every single night you go out, progress farther along the path to being more confident in yourself, and therefore more successful with men—just as you become less dependent on them to make you feel valued for who you are.

We'll show you what that means, step by step, from choosing what you put on to how to make your approach. (We'll even teach you how to be your own best bartender, from mastering recipes to learning bar folklore.) But unlike other dating books out there that ask you to go shopping for a new wardrobe, or adopt personality traits that are totally foreign to you, we're going to keep reminding you that every tool you need is inside of you. The right clothes are already hanging in your

closet; all the charm and wit and silliness you need to attract people this very minute is within you. You are already perfect, just as you are. And if that makes you roll
your eyes and think, "Yeah, right—I'm still the chubby
seventh-grade girl with braces on her teeth," keep reading. Cancel your magazine subscriptions, throw away all
of those dumb self-help books, stop paying your psychic
astrologer, don't call your friend who hasn't gotten a
date in five years. Why? Because they're all wrong. They
don't know you as well as you know yourself, and they
certainly don't know the workings of your heart.

There are millions of men out there, all with different tastes and wants and desires. And all you need to
do to meet some of them, to enjoy your interactions
with them, is to put your best foot forward. Because of
our experience, we can suggest how you might do that
so that you don't get lost in a crowded, noisy bar where
people may not have the time or inclination to get to
know the "real" you.

We can help you feel more in control in a bar. We
can help you learn how to end every single night exactly the way you want it to end. And in doing so, our
bet is you will feel more in control of yourself. Yeah, a
bar is a place where you can let your guard down and

have a good time. But a bar is also a microcosm of the world, and if you can learn how to feel in charge there, you can learn to feel in charge of almost every area of your life. The key is to be conscious of decisions you make unknowingly every day, from your habitual drinking of coffee to your reactions to old Achilles' heels. To learn to be awake, to be aware, to listen, and to be decisive.

Knowing how to walk into a strange bar with confidence and ease will make walking into a job interview easier. Learning how to be warm and inviting, even when you're feeling scared, will make any blind date or solo outing less stressful. Learning to say no when you've had enough to drink will help you set limits in the rest of your life, as well. If you can open yourself to the fun of the bar scene, you're halfway to recognizing the fun of life. It's something that so many people have trouble with—recognizing the possibility of joy in the everyday, yours to be had for the taking.

We want you to be able to conquer men if that's what you're after, or to feel comfortable in your own skin when you're pulling up a stool next to your best friend. The point is, if you can learn to get comfortable in a public, social setting like a bar, the world can be your martini glass.

You Can Use Your Insecurity to Your Advantage

It always makes us laugh when women confide in us, "I'm so uncomfortable in a bar. My friends seem so at ease, but I can't quite figure it out." We're laughing with compassion, because we know something our female clients don't: Everyone feels uncomfortable on first walking into a social situation. That's why so many people drink too much: to take the edge off the shyness. We don't know a single woman out there who doesn't experience nights of feeling shy, or unattractive, or like the only fraud in the room who's faking it while everyone else seems to naturally understand exactly what's going on. As one of our women friends said the other night, "It's like everyone else has gotten the rule book to life, and now Amazon.com is all sold out."

Sure, some people are more comfortable than others in a social setting, but no one, and we mean *no one*, is comfortable going to a bar and looking for love. Going out with your friends to grab a drink? Of course. Visiting your local bartending friend to catch up? Absolutely. But there isn't a woman or man out there who walks into a public place hoping to attract attention who isn't also worried about not getting any at all, or worse, about getting the wrong kind. That someone will have the power to look into their deepest soul, and in the time it takes to finish off a beer, see everything that's wrong with them.

But here's a newsflash, and it's a comforting one: Unless you sit there rocking back and forth on your bar stool having a conversation with your invisible friend while sucking your thumb, no one is going to think you're a loser. It's not going to occur to *us*, because we, your bartenders, are too busy working, and it's not going to occur to the men sitting there beside you, because they're too worried about their own insecurities. Plus, there are plenty of men who are interested in shy women, who find comfort in them. As one customer told us, "A girl who looks shy and reserved in a crowded, noisy room is intriguing to me. It means she's probably watching the room like I am."

There's only one way a guy is going to pick up on your insecurity, and that's if you announce it. Which you're not going to do, because you are an adult. And as an adult in a public place, you know how to act, even if you sometimes feel unsteady. There has never been one single time that a man has approached you and you actually *did* throw up. Remember: Feelings aren't facts. And even at your most painfully insecure, there are still ways that you can make insecurity work to your advantage. Not to mention several easy ways to distract yourself and others from the momentary reality of how you're feeling.

A Smile's Worth a Thousand Words

Honestly. A genuine, open smile is the most attractive accessory a woman can have, especially if it's aimed in a man's direction, or he's the reason why that smile is there. Just the other night we watched this woman who walked into the bar, clearly not feeling her best.

Tools You'll Need to Be a Cocktail-Making Queen

1. **Proper glassware** Make sure to always have on hand an assortment of wineglasses, champagne flutes, martini glasses, and "rocks" glasses in which to serve cocktails over ice.

2. **A Boston shaker** This is a 16-ounce shaker, which is used as a mixing glass, and a 22-ounce metal "can" that fits around it as a top (and is a mixing glass in its own right). Since the shaker is smaller than the top, remember never to fill it to the rim!

3. **A julep strainer** This is a large perforated spoon that fits over the 22-ounce metal top of the Boston shaker.

4. **A spring strainer, or Hawthorne strainer** This strainer fits around the 22-ounce metal top of the Boston shaker, but it has a spring attached.

5. **A bar spoon** A 12-inch spoon with a spiral handle that you can use for stirring as well as measuring.

6. **A muddler** You'll want this to crush fruits, herbs, and sugar. Make sure it is 6 inches long so it can reach to the bottom of the Boston shaker.

7. **A paring knife** You'll use this to cut fruits and twists. It will

work best if you reserve it for these purposes only so it stays extremely sharp.

8. **A jigger** Think of a jigger as a shot glass, all grown up. A jigger is used to measure liquor into a drink and looks like two cones joined at their points.

9. **A can opener and church key** This is a can opener on one end and a bottle opener on the other.

10. **A wine opener** We suggest you make the investment in a wine opener that has a two-stage opening process, rather than the simple twist-in-pull-out kind. The two-stagers help preserve the corks, especially those of French wines, which tend to be extra long.

11. **A grater** Delegate one for bar purposes only so no cheese gets mixed in with your lemon zest or nutmeg!

Her shoulders were slumped, and she spent a lot of time looking at the floor. One man started to talk to her and for the first few minutes, we were worried she was going to lose his attention if she didn't say a word. But then he said something to make her smile, and that smile just lit up the room. In that moment, we turned our backs because we knew the two of them would be just fine. He was pleased at being able to make her feel happy, and she forgot that she hadn't been feeling so great. She allowed herself to find pleasure in him, and in the moment, and it showed. She was able to be magnetic even when she wasn't necessarily feeling it.

We recently did a casual poll in our bar about what turned men on, other than the usual *Baywatch* fantasy. And every single one of the men—*every single one*—put a smile at the top of their list. If you could only begin to understand (which we hope you will soon!) how incredibly insecure men are, your emotional reaction to them in a bar, or in the world, would be so much less infused with drama. Men are constantly terrified that they're not good enough. So even if you're not sure what to say to let them know you're interested in starting or continuing a conversation, all you need to do is throw them one sweet, encouraging smile. We promise they'll be yours, even if just for the moment.

Remember: Men Like to Chase

It may be painful to be shy, but with men, shy can actually always trump sophisticated. (Sophisticated tends to be a quality men don't really understand, anyway.) Men *want* to approach you; they just need a signal to know it's OK. Every guy at the bar tells us all he wants is permission to say hi to the woman who seems attractive or nice—"nice" equaling "attractive" far more often than you might imagine. If you think you could be interested in a guy, all you need to do is give him some encouragement.

You don't have to be the wit of the party. And you certainly don't need to be Dorothy Parker at the vicious roundtable. Indeed, it's our hope that you'll avoid "viciousness" at all costs.

As long as you are friendly (back to that ready smile), no man is going to be put off by the fact that you seem quiet. In fact, most will take it as a challenge to draw you out. Understand this: Whatever panic circuits are shorting out in your head, most men read shy as demure or feminine, not as terrified. And men are egocentric enough to think that you have spent your lifetime, shy person that you are, just *waiting* for him to come along and draw you out. Men are already scared of you just by virtue of the fact that you're a woman, so any sign of humanity—from a spilled drink to a chink in your armor—can be a wonderfully comforting thing for them.

For instance: Your worst nightmare from high school, told with humor, can be very reassuring for a man to hear. The fact that you don't take your every perceived fault seriously is important in creating intimacy. The ability to laugh at yourself allows for him to believe that you'll find his faults equally humorous in a compassionate, nonjudgmental way. Angelina Jolie may be one of the most beautiful women on earth, but ask most guys if they'd like to actually meet her for dinner, and we guarantee that they'd panic. The women men masturbate to may be airbrushed, but the women they love are flawed.

It's true. Whatever patina of sophistication you may be going for, chances are good it's going to be appreciated by your women friends or no one at all. Because the reality is that men *love* unjaded women. Our friend Liza comes across as what some might label a "man-eater." She is beautiful and sexy; she radiates intelligence and confidence, with the killer body language that goes along with that image of "perfection." In other words, she's set up to get every guy she desires. But in fact, she is alone and lonely. She sits with us at the bar some nights and washes away that loneliness with champagne. Because what we didn't mention is that in addition to all of her attributes, she is jaded and hardened. She doesn't have a sense of humor about herself. She isn't able to laugh at the fact that we're all full of bullshit, and we're just trying to do the best we can every day. Hopefully a little better than we did the day before, and that's worth cheering. But after learning that this "perfect" woman is actually shut down to any kind of joy, men don't even want to stick around for Liza's beauty. She's just too hard to seduce. What you might think of as unsophisticated and naive might actually be a positive part of you—the part that is open to joy and possibility.

Now that we've got that straight, the next time a guy you find appealing tries to pick you up, no matter how shy the whole thing may make you, take a deep breath and try to allow him to do it, despite your nervousness.

Stock Up! The Bare Basics of a Liquor Cabinet

1. **Simple syrup** Keeps indefinitely in the refrigerator. Sugar water is used in scores of sweetened cocktails. To make simple syrup, mix equal parts regular sugar and hot water and then cool; superfine sugar will dissolve immediately in room temperature water.

2. **Vodka** Choose one of a decent quality. It shouldn't come in a plastic bottle. Vodka's the perfect staple because it can be mixed with everyday ingredients like club soda, or orange or cranberry juice.

3. **Gin** Look for a London dry gin, which tends to be the best (Beefeater and Tanqueray are two classics). If you want a lower alcohol content, try Plymouth gin, which has a lower proof than most of its peers.

4. **Dry vermouth** Making martinis is so easy and helps turn everything into a celebration. Vermouth is generally not that expensive. Try Noilly Prat dry vermouth.

5. **Whiskey** Even more than with other alcohols, your choice of whiskey should really be determined by your personal taste. Do you like scotch or bourbon? If you're using whiskey to

make cocktails rather than to sip neat or on the rocks, Wild Turkey rye whiskey is great.

6. **Rum** There are two kinds of rums: those that are meant to be sipped, like a fine scotch, and those that are meant to be used in mixed drinks like rum and Coke, or daiquiris. One that swings both ways is 10 Cane, which is of high enough quality to sip but inexpensive enough to mix.

7. **Tequila** Tequila's generally drunk either as a shot or in a margarita. Be careful not to use your very expensive, sipping tequila in a margarita or you'll find yourself with an empty bottle before you know it!

8. **Angostura bitters** Bitters are a classic part of mixology and the key to a good Manhattan. You can find them in your supermarket along with other mixers.

You may just be showing off one of your greatest assets. As one buddy says, "Shy women can totally be sexy in their very shyness, because they have their own form of attitude that translates like this: They may act coy and demure, but beneath it they have a secret confidence they want you to know about." See what we're saying? Men may not get women, but sometimes they don't get them in ways that only work to your advantage!

In Your Silence, You Fuel Men's Imaginations

If you find you're unable to say much about yourself at first, you can use your reserve merely by turning the attention to the guy you're talking with. All you need to do is ask the man you're talking to a couple of questions about himself so that the conversation can keep going. Since we all like to talk about ourselves, this can work out perfectly: The guy gets to chatter away about whatever it is he finds most interesting about himself, and you have a chance to take a deep breath and get your bearings.

We're going to talk later about the kinds of questions that make most men respond with the greatest ease and openness, but in general it's difficult to go wrong if you keep turning the conversation back to them. That's really the perfect party trick for even the shiest woman.

We have one customer who actually *is* a rock star and recently admitted to us that she's painfully shy. We couldn't believe it—she dresses like she could give lessons in hotness, and she never radiates anything but confidence. We asked her how she manages to portray the opposite of what she's actually feeling and she said, "I just never let it get the best of me. It's always painful at the beginning, but I find that if I start to ask people questions about themselves, I forget about myself. Because I'm really interested in other people, and as they start talking about themselves, I forget about myself and how scared I am."

Why Is That Guy Out?

It's not a hard-and-fast science—alas, there is no grand data bank that can tell us how many people hook up in a bar, or even marry the people they hook up with in a bar—but since we are on the front lines, we asked our customers, both regulars and first-timers, why they go out. What we heard again and again is that people go out to escape the boredom of everyday life, and to have an experience that is exciting, or at least different from the usual grind. But what they're looking for after that is as random and unique as the people we polled. Why are they out?

> To relax: 37%
>
> To check out the scene: 27%
>
> To drink: 15%
>
> To meet somebody: 13%
>
> To sample the food: 5%
>
> Miscellaneous: 3%

Cocktail

The **KIR ROYAL** offers confidence in every sip. It's easy to make, easy to drink, and beautiful to look at. For one serving, you'll need:

Splash of crème de cassis

Enough chilled champagne or sparkling wine to fill a flute

Pour a splash of crème de cassis into a champagne flute (you can always add more if you like). Holding the glass at an angle so as to preserve the alcohol's carbonation, slowly add the champagne or wine.

Honesty with Yourself Is the *Only* Policy

*L*et's just start with the basic, hard truth: Everyone makes up stories. We do it when we think that someone else's life is glamorous and perfect, or when we daydream about what our boss's home life is like, or when we fantasize about what someone we met quickly is *really* like. But we also tell ourselves stories about ourselves. Usually, we're making up things we want to believe, like "If only I lost five pounds/fell in love/got promoted at work, everything would be perfect." Not true, of course, but relatively harmless.

Unfortunately, all too often we make up things

about ourselves that aren't true, and then buy into it. "He'll never like me because . . ." or "I'm not a lovable person." That means that we spend a lot of time telling ourselves lies. Sometimes, those lies are nice. But most of the time—and we think this is true more for women than men, since you spend much more time analyzing yourselves and your place in the world—the lies we tell ourselves are really, really nasty. You convince yourself, for a myriad of reasons, that you're a failure who no one will ever love—not once they get to know the real you.

The problem with thinking like this isn't just that you spend nights obsessing about the wrong stuff, when you could be, we dunno, organizing your lingerie drawer. It's that by spending so much time pretending that you're someone else, you're convincing yourself and everyone around you that *this* is really who you are. This can be a very powerful, positive thing when it reflects well on you. Many of the world's great beauties aren't textbook classic lookers but radiate a confidence they've spent years building up. But when you turn your story *back* on yourself, you're running the serious risk of showing the world that you're something less than you are. Feel awful enough about yourself, be unkind to yourself, and that's what men will respond to.

Here's an example we see all the time. It's stupid, and it's base. But chances are, if you're like our female customers, you may have experienced this once or twice. You think you have cellulite. Said imagined cellulite makes you feel completely crazy. You change the way you dress. You nervously feel your thighs at odd moments to make sure none has suddenly sprouted there at the last minute. You even (tragic to say, but true), talk about it to men. And here's why the whole thing is so sad and pathetic and damaging: Men don't give a shit if you have cellulite. Most of them don't notice, and of those who do, most don't care. Hell, if you're sleeping with a guy, chances are he's so damn grateful he's not spending his time checking out the space between your butt and your leg where you're convinced wrinkles of fat are making their home. And you know what? They may even *like* it. Very few men like anorexic women, and even if they feel they should be dating someone who looks thin, a major percentage of those men will admit they close their eyes and imagine having something to hold on to.

What men *do* care about is that you're radiating insecurity. Again, *this is not about how you're acting a month into the relationship.* Date number two, be who you are. This is about the first two hours you spend with a guy in a place so crowded, and so filled with distractions, that there's no time to make much more than a first impression.

So what he's seeing is that you're dressing in a way that you think hides your invisible cellulite, but to him just looks dowdy. You keep grabbing your leg—what, do you have fleas? And God forbid you ask him if he sees what you see . . . you've just taken him from a place of complete happiness (that he's getting close to this gorgeous young thing) to a place of wondering who you are and what the hell is wrong with you. Remember, while women may find other women's overt insecurity par for the course, a guy in the bar isn't necessarily going to peg what it is and then flip on the compassion switch.

Men are very, very simple creatures (although you probably suspect this already). They don't get layers. And they certainly don't stick around long enough to peel off those layers to get to the "true you" the way women do with their girlfriends. Men smell your lies and they run. Unless—again, this is one of those things you aren't necessarily going to like—you're exactly their physical type, in which case they'll be happy to stick around and try to hook up with you. But even then, chances are slim they'll be there for breakfast.

Which is why it always comes back to the all-important job of figuring out who you are. That doesn't need to be as complicated as it sounds. We don't mean who you are spiritually, or what kind of woman you want to be, or why your parents made you this way or that way. It would be great if you could start asking and answering those questions, but as far as next weekend is concerned, keep it simple. Be honest about where you are, right now. If you are 5 feet 2 inches, stop obsessing about the kind of woman you'd be if you had a supermodel's legs. It ain't never gonna happen. That doesn't mean men don't think you're hot. If you're bubbly and funny, that's cool, too—but don't pretend to be Greta Garbo. And if you're Greta Garbo, please don't try to be bubbly and funny. That just confuses and scares people.

The point is that just as there are many types of women, there are just as many men who like each and every single one of those types. "Be true to yourself" is a cliché for a reason. It works. People who are comfortable with themselves make other people feel comfortable. Men are simple, but they're not (all) stupid. If you pretend to be someone you're not, trust us, men will be on to you. And they don't like to be manipulated or deceived any more than the next person.

So skip faking it. You may fool yourself, but you probably won't fool other people. And even if you do, it will result in joylessness. So take the time you need to take stock. Write down ten things you really like about yourself. Memorize them, and celebrate them. And for God's sake, throw out that other list—the bad one—*immediately.* It's a total fantasy, and we'd bet the bar that it's just plain wrong.

Feelings Aren't Facts

Think the story you're telling yourself about who you are is what you're projecting into the world? That just isn't the case 99 percent of the time. We asked various women what they were feeling insecure about that night. Then we asked a guy next to them what they thought about those qualities and how they might be used to the women's advantage.

She said: "I'm feeling shy."

He said: "A bar scene can be daunting, so I like that she's acknowledging that. I know I get a little nervous when I'm approaching someone in a bar. But if she *stays* really shy once I've been talking to her for a while, that could be a problem because it can come across as being shut down or cold. She can totally counteract that, though, just by being warm—smiling at me, or buying me a drink. Something to signal she's interested."

She said: "I overthink everything."

He said: "Honestly, as long as she isn't busy overthinking me to my face, that doesn't bother me. It could definitely get tiring if she needs to analyze everything that's going on around her in a social situation, but what she does in her own head isn't my business. And it might make her interesting to be in a relationship with, or at least more interesting than a woman who doesn't think about anything!"

She said: "I talk too much."

He said: "Well . . . that's a tough one. If she *does* in fact talk too much, that could make me nuts. But maybe her idea of 'too much' is my idea of someone who's involved in the conversation. I guess I'd want her to read my face, and if she feels like she's talking too much, to be quiet for a bit. It's not like it's something that she can't control, depending on the situation."

She said: "The wrong thing always comes out of my mouth."

He said: "If she's funny about it, and I feel like she's just being honest as opposed to playing coy or by some stupid rules she thinks she's supposed to be following, that's cool. If the 'wrong thing' means 'super critical,' forget it, but it can be really cute when a woman says what comes into her mind and doesn't edit herself."

She said: "I'm too intense."

He said: "Like, stalker intense? Or crazy-in-bed-let's-do-it-on-the-kitchen-counter intense? Because that one is *not* a fine line. If she's writing off mental illness as intensity, I'm outta here. But if what she's talking about is being passionate, I'd like to see some of that!"

She said: "I'm not sexy."

He said: "Honey, you're a woman. That makes you sexy right there."

Cocktail

Just as nothing says "girl" better than a drink that comes with an umbrella sticking out of it, nothing says "woman" more than an elegant cocktail. And there's nothing more sophisticated than a classic **GIN MARTINI**. For one drink, you'll need:

3 ounces Tanqueray gin
½ ounce Noilly Prat dry vermouth
Olive or lemon twist

Pour the gin and vermouth into a mixing glass. Add ice and stir until the outside of the glass is cool to the touch. Strain into a chilled martini glass and garnish with an olive or a twist.

Typecast Yourself First and No One Else Can

We, as well as most men, understand women. And we get, as well as you do, that you are seriously complicated. Crazy complicated. Which means that on any given night, you can feel like showing off a different part of yourself. All we're asking, as the bartenders who are watching the night play out, is for you to be honest with yourself—before you even get in the shower— about how you're feeling about yourself *on this particular night*. What element of your personality are you likely to be putting on display? Because just as there are some very simple categories, the reactions men have to the "categories" are equally simple.

We all tend to whittle ourselves down to a type in a bar—and for good reason. It's not as if this is the place to show off the subtle things that make up the beautiful uniqueness of who you are. Indeed, it should take a man—just as it has taken your best women friends— months, if not years, to understand all the complicated parts of you that make you so beloved to them.

We've broken down the "types" we see the most often—and we haven't met a woman who hasn't, at some point, embodied all of them. Which is why we're betting they'll all sound familiar to you. The point of doing this is to keep the archetypes in mind so you might know how, on the night in question, you are coming across to other people. And while we're giving "cons" to these parts of your personality, what we intend to do is simply point out that when you play to that one personality type, guys may read you merely based upon what they see.

Use it to your advantage, but as always, also take responsibility for what you're putting out there.

Tinker Bell

She flits, she floats, she works her fairy-dust magic.

PROS She's dynamic. She's irresistible. When you're

feeling like Tinker Bell, heads turn when you laugh, and men want to get closer. One of our favorite Tinker Bells (and believe us, we've seen her on days when she isn't at her Tinker Belliest!) comes into the bar determined to have a good time no matter what. Regardless of what work has dealt her, she always wears a smile and exudes genuine warmth. Even when she's just there with her girlfriends, it never fails that guys look up from across the room, drawn by her sparkle.

CONS Watch the flapping of those wings, sister. Recently, we watched a woman who was in the bar with a couple of friends. She and this guy across the room made eye contact and smiled at each other, and you could see that there was definitely a connection. But while the guy sat there for a few minutes, just biding his time until it was a good moment to get over there and talk to her, she suddenly started playing to the crowd, thinking she had to do more to reel him in. While he'd been intrigued watching her laugh and joke naturally with her friends, suddenly she was screaming, she was ordering shots, she was telling jokes too loudly. It wasn't long before the guy turned back to his friends. She hadn't realized that getting his attention in the first place was all she had to do and he just needed time to get comfortable to approach her.

The Accidental Temptress

This is you when you're feeling the most comfortable with yourself. You are the accidental temptress those nights when you don't have an agenda—or if you do, you're not going to let it get in the way of having a good time.

PROS The accidental temptress, when she's good, is perfect. Our favorite example is this woman who is luckier with men than anyone has a right to be. This woman slays. Everyone wants to be with her. She flies to Paris for weekends, and she's gotten a marriage offer from an actual prince. And here is the honest truth: She is perfectly average-looking. We mean *average*. Not a single person ever turns around on the street when she walks by, because there is nothing worth looking at—physically, at least, when you first get a glimpse of her—that demands you look twice. But she is so completely comfortable with who she is that everyone wants to be with her, because everyone, from women to men to dogs, feels easy around her. She never lies about being brilliant, or about having extra degrees, or about owning a house in the country. She's just herself, without pretense, and that fact alone makes her absolutely extraordinary.

CONS One misstep and the temptress part goes flying out the window, leaving men feeling as if they're sitting with their sister or favorite cousin. Sure, they'll buy that girl a drink, but then they'll slap her on the back and challenge her to a game of darts. Slip, and you go from tempting to milquetoast.

The Pleaser

You're the pleaser when you're feeling a little shaky about yourself. That doesn't mean you can't perform, but you'll do anything you have to, to the point of desperation, to win acceptance.

PROS When you're feeling like the pleaser, you'll go out of your way to engage in conversations with strangers. Even though you're feeling insecure, you're desperate to feel better about yourself, and the best way to do that is have a stranger respond to you. The pleaser, when she comes out, can make some interesting connections at the bar, even if it's just meeting someone who might be a friend. The pleaser is also often generous: One customer, just the other week, heard that we

were putting together a benefit and automatically offered to help, which was invaluable, since she owned a
stationery company that could make the invitations.

CONS The pleaser can get into real trouble because
she forgets about herself in her effort to be accommo-
dating. This means she is the one willing to go along
with a conversation and try to participate in it, when
she has absolutely no idea what the guy is talking
about. Instead of having the confidence to say, "Oh,
tell me about that restaurant, I haven't heard of it," or
"Where is that hotel again?" the pleaser nods away,
even when the guy is asking her if she's been there.
And then, boom! Total embarrassment is always just a
step away because she's inevitably busted, and then
panics because she looks like a liar. It's always, always
better to be honest. The guy might be thrilled to have
a chance to tell you something you don't know.

The Sharer

Your guard is down, you're psyched to be out, you're
feeling one with your fellow man.

PROS The sharer can be hilarious company—chatty,
straightforward, telling her funniest stories. When
you're in your sharer mode, and you're at your best,

Bar Myths: Bad Luck Omens and Faux Pas

We all worry about how to start talking to strangers: too personal is . . . too personal; asking for astrological signs went out thirty years ago. But facts are always fun—especially if they're about drinking. Doubt us? Read on.

1. An even number of olives in your martini is bad luck. Either one or three olives is the appropriate amount. This myth may have come from the old Italian custom of putting three espresso beans in a glass of sambuca for good luck.

2. Lighting your cigarette from a candle is bad luck (not to mention bad form). This may come from the old saying that every time a cigarette was lit from a candle a sailor died (sailors used to sell matches to supplement their incomes, so not using matches was denying them money).

3. Lighting three cigarettes from one match or lighter flick is bad luck. This comes from World War I, when soldiers believed that in the time it took to light three cigarettes in a row in the trenches, the enemy could track their location.

4. You'll have seven years of bad sex if you don't look people in the eyes when you clink glasses with them. (Bad sex or not, it's

poor form not to look the person in the eye who is toasting your health, happiness, or friendship.)

5. It is a faux pas to order a martini or cosmopolitan in a "regular" or rocks glass. You may say, "But I can't hold the glass without spilling it!" Take the first few sips out of it while it sits on the bar, or just load up on napkins.

men will automatically gravitate toward you because you're hilarious and open. You let men forget that women are ultimately terrifying to them. Plus, we love a good "and then I did something really, really naughty" story, both as bartenders and men. One of our best female friends comes in every Sunday, sidles up the bar, and amuses us with her dating stories from the weekend. She's funnier and more honest than any of the characters on *Sex and the City*.

CONS While we're saying you should be who you are, we're not suggesting for a second that you walk into a bar and start spilling every insecurity you've managed to accumulate over the years. The bar is still a public place, which means you should always show yourself in the most positive light possible. There's a huge difference between selling out and marketing your best points. Just as you wouldn't tell your job interviewer that you failed Econ 101 because you were in the middle of a horrible breakup (hey, you graduated, didn't you—and with a good cume, too), you shouldn't march into a bar and start talking about how miserably uncomfortable you are at a bar, talking to a stranger, and how unhappy you are being single.

And Who Are You, My Dear?

1. **You walk past a construction site and get catcalled. You respond by:**
   a. Blushing and pretending it isn't happening (1 point)
   b. Looking up and smiling (2 points)
   c. Waving and saying, "Thanks, guys!" (3 points)

2. **You pick up a copy of *Vogue*. You wonder:**
   a. If you can copy the designs you like on your sewing machine (1 point)
   b. Who you know who can get you a discount (2 points)
   c. If "max" on your credit card *really* stands for "maximum" (3 points)

3. **You're late for work, your stockings run, you can't find your keys. You:**
   a. Retreat to bed with a box of bonbons and call all your friends to share your woes (1 point)
   b. Call the locksmith and head out the door—you have a job to do (2 points)
   c. Whip out the least-maxed-out credit card and buy yourself a mink (3 points)

4. **Your best friend is dumped by her boyfriend. You:**

a. Book a mani/pedi for both of you during lunch (1 point)

b. Send her a gift certificate for a mani/pedi for whenever she wants (2 points)

c. Arrange for a male stripper to surprise her at her house (3 points)

5. You're dumped by your boyfriend. You:

a. Call your mother (1 point)

b. Call your best friend (2 points)

c. Head to the nearest bar and pick up another guy to distract you (3 points)

RESULTS:

5–7 points: Honey, you've got a heart as big as they come. But you could think about saving a little bit of it for yourself and remembering some of the many reasons you deserve to feel confident and strong.

8–12: When you're on your game, you score like no one else. Just make sure to notice when you're heading toward the goal line so you can stay in control.

13–15: You dazzle. But if you see the people around you putting on their shades, you might want to turn the wattage down just a bit.

Cocktail

You've got a strong character, and so does a **MANHATTAN**. It's a bold, old-fashioned drink that we've tinkered with a bit so that it doesn't burn so much going down. For one drink, you'll need:

1½ ounces Wild Turkey rye whiskey

1 ounce Cinzano sweet vermouth

½ ounce Grand Marnier

3 dashes of Angostura bitters

Lemon twist

Combine all the ingredients in a mixing glass. Add ice and stir until the outside of the glass is cool to the touch. Strain into a cocktail glass or a martini glass and garnish with a twist.

You Have to Know What You Want in Order to Get It

OK, so far you're ahead. You're being honest about how you're feeling about yourself, and you've got a handle on who exactly it is you want to meet.

So now ask yourself this question: What is it you're after on this particular night?

Go ahead—be brutally honest. No one can hear you. But you definitely need to hear yourself. Because the second you decide on your intention, you begin setting things into action. Which means you start setting up for the consequences. And since the only thing that really matters is being responsible for yourself, feeling *good* about yourself and your decisions, this is really important. Imagine the liberation that is possible when you don't wake up a single morning thinking, "What did I do?" Sure, you may have screwed up. But at least be able to know you took that risk, and then you'll be in a position to laugh about it .

Here's what you need to know, from yourself, for yourself, in order to feel good about the consequences, no matter what they are. *Why are you going out, and what do you want to take away from your experience?* Are you craving attention because you're feeling insecure? If that's the case, be aware, before the night begins, that feeling insecure can make you more vulnerable than usual, because you might be too quick to respond to attention. Do you want to go out and kiss someone? If so, make sure to make a note to yourself, while you're still sober and before you even meet the guy, that all you want to do is kiss. That can stop you from being in a compromising position. Do you want to go out and take someone to bed? That's your business, but again, it's important to know in your heart, before you do anything else, what it is you're after. This can be such an enormous antidote to the painful regret we've all felt too many times the day after, when we've just let the evening "happen."

One good trick is to close your eyes for a moment and visualize the night unfolding in a realistic way that would make you comfortable. Are you laughing with your friends? Having a deep conversation with a stranger? When you open your door later that night, how do you want to feel? Do you want to be sober? Alone? Can you feel good about being alone, because you still had fun?

Now do the opposite. Think about what your downfalls tend to be. Do you drink too much? End up making out with guys you don't like? Close your eyes and see that happening, and remember how it makes you feel. Tell yourself that's not how you want to feel at the end of *this* evening. See the story in your mind, and catch yourself when you see something you don't like. Maybe you see yourself coming home too late, when you have a morning meeting. *This* is the time to change the story, not when it's actually happening. This is always when we hear the heartbreak across the bar, the times when a night or an interaction hasn't gone along with the fairy tale that many women seem to believe is their right. Hey—we love men. But seldom are they able to show up to play the fantasy part that is in your head.

We'd love for you to prove us wrong. But mostly, we want you to always, *always* feel in control of the choices you are making, from before you set foot out of your house to the moment you return home again. So take a quiet moment—when you're in the shower, or changing your clothes, or walking your dog—and think about your agenda. You have nothing to prove. And if you are out to prove something, you aren't being true to yourself or your goals.

You're Looking for Love

You really, really want a boyfriend. You want it the way most men want a new Porsche. Now, we're not saying it isn't possible to find that person in a bar on a Friday night. Hell, if we didn't believe anything was possible in a bar, we wouldn't be able to do what we do. But remember, *it's a bar.*

The chances of meeting the person who is going to be your soul mate fifty years from now are pretty slim. What we're about to tell you may make you feel like you're walking into a locker room uninvited and invisible, but know it as the truth: Most of the men we talk to feel like if they're at a bar, and you're at a bar, you're both looking to hook up. End of story. We're sure you know this, but in case you need reminding, going out and meeting someone is *not* the same as dating. Never make any assumptions when you go out that you're going to meet a boyfriend. Going out is a social activity, and a social activity only.

We're not discouraging you from being open to the potential for more—we *want* that for you—but you shouldn't bank on it, or be disappointed if it doesn't happen. Because then the whole night's a bust, when if you'd just been able to enjoy what was in front of you, even if it was an old friend, you might have had a great night. You should be able, no matter who you are, to leave a night at a bar feeling empowered, attractive, and successful. Whatever happens after that is only about frosting the cake.

Approach a night in the bar exactly the way you try to approach life: by being in the present, being grateful for whatever good comes your way, and by having fun as it unfolds. Forget about keeping score of what you want but you're not getting. So the dude next to you is so unattractive you could never, ever imagine kissing him. But maybe he's a great dart player, or he would be perfect for your cousin. Whether you are out for the night, on a vacation, or even sitting in a meeting, try to find something to enjoy about where you are and what's happening. The benefits of really trying to live like this are twofold: You'll be much happier. And because you're happier, more men will want to be with you. Men are terrified of women who hope, think, or count on a man to make them whole.

You're Looking for Friendship

You're going out to catch up with an old friend. That's great. But now stop for a minute before you go any further in your planning. If what you really want is just to hang out with a friend, think about what you're wearing and where you are going with particular care (more on how to do that later). Because nothing is going to be more annoying to you or your friend than if you're constantly interrupted by guys who think you're out there and looking.

Also, make sure your friend is on board with the plan. We watched this one pair of girlfriends go from friends for life to never speaking again. And that's because one of the pair, who was recently divorced, convinced herself—and her friend—that what she really needed was some time with her best friend. But as the night went on, the recently divorced woman would start looking around the room. She talked to every guy who sent her a drink, while she left her friend to just look on. She said she was going to the bathroom and then she wouldn't come back for twenty minutes because she was talking to someone else, while her best friend just sat there by herself. The moral of this story? Don't let something ugly like desperation compromise who you are and what you think is important.

You're Looking to Get Laid

Don't even *think* about blushing when you read that line. Trust us—it is the number one reason we see most women coming into our bar every night. Maybe you don't want to get laid that particular night, right off the bat, but you're hoping to have a good make-out and set something in motion where you will get laid soon.

Be honest, because you can put yourself in a bad position if you give off a signal that is different from the one you intend to give off. And you really need to be as honest as you can be about your intentions with the friends who are with you, because if you're going to leave the bar with a stranger with the intention of hooking up, someone in your crowd needs to know his name, or something about him, just to make sure you're covered. And forgive us if we're preaching to the converted, but there are still some sinners out there: Please, please carry condoms. And use them. A woman is just as responsible, from our point of view, for making sure that guys wear them as the guy is. If not more so, since you're the one who can end up pregnant.

You're Looking to Forget, or You're Bored

From our point of view, these are the scariest emotional places a woman can be when it comes to how her night plays out. This is when you're likely to have too much to drink and end up throwing up or weeping over nothing. Or at least feeling like crap the next day. (Or doing something really, really stupid *and* feeling like crap the next day.) Hey—it's totally cool to head out to a bar in order to meet new people, or to forget about the guy who never called you back, or to distract yourself from the mean boss who is making your life hell. But be honest about it with yourself and realize that since your attitude is one that makes you think you have nothing to lose, you may be a little less conscientious than you normally would be on a night when you're feeling better about yourself and your life.

If this is the case, think about going to a bar close to your house so you can get home easily and without relying on anyone else. Consider going with a good friend who knows what's going on in your head. And *please* watch what you drink. Customers who are unhappy or bored usually want a drink (or drinks) more than anyone else in the room, but they're also the customers who need to keep more of a lid on things, since they're feeling a little more out of control even before they've felt the effects of alcohol.

We're not judging you for a second. We're just asking you to be responsible for your own emotional well-being. It's something that even the most confident of women can struggle with on certain nights. Just recently, we watched it happen with one of our best customers, a woman who's self-assured, accomplished, and funny—basically, a thoroughly modern woman in her thirties. She's got quite the sex drive on her, and she doesn't need to apologize for it. But the other night, she came into our bar after a really hard day at work. She'd lost an account and was feeling bad about herself. She joked with us that if she was a guy, all it would take to feel better was scoring with someone, and goddamn it, that's what she was going to do. She was going to hit her mark, and she was going to feel good about it.

Instead, by the end of the night, she was feeling lonely and even worse about herself. Sure, she had ten phone numbers in her pocket, but told us that instead of that boosting her confidence, she just felt cheap. She had ten phone numbers of guys who wanted her to call when she left the bar and meet them somewhere, but that didn't make her feel happy for a second.

She was lucky, because she kept in control and didn't follow through with any of the men. And she was lucky because she realized she was headed down the wrong path that night, rather than the next morning when she woke up to find herself in someone else's bed. But she could have saved herself one hell of an annoying time of it if she'd figured it out before she left home and just came in to hang out with us.

Confidence Check List

Keep these ten things in mind as you go through your evening, and occasionally check back in and see how you're doing. Try to make sure to:

1. Don't forget your intent
2. Be happy where you are, or go somewhere else
3. Remind yourself you are rarely the exception, and keep your expectations realistic
4. Eat something
5. Think before you speak as often as possible
6. Stay positive about yourself and the people around you
7. Know your alcohol limit, and stick to it
8. Remember this is about fun
9. Stay true to yourself, no matter what you think the guy next to you is looking for
10. Adore the bartender!

Cocktail

Learning what you want doesn't need to be complicated, and it can be *so* very rewarding. Just like a CHAMPAGNE COCKTAIL! For one drink, you'll need:

Sugar cube

3 dashes Angostura bitters

Enough Champagne or sparkling wine to fill a flute

Lemon twist

Place a sugar cube at the bottom of a champagne flute. Add the bitters. Slowly pour champagne to the top of the angled glass, taking your time, since the bitters and sugar will make the champagne bubble up very quickly. Garnish with a lemon twist.

A Wingman Can Be Your Best Accessory

You're feeling good, you're looking good, and you're gonna get lucky—whatever that entails for you at this particular moment. But assuming you're not taking yourself out to the local diner for a grilled cheese, it's all about the company.

For your own joy, first and foremost. But also because if you're looking to attract a certain kind of man, it's really important to think about the person who will be seated on the bar stool next to you.

You cannot begin to overestimate the importance of your wingman. Not just because your fun depends on it in case nothing else happens that night other than the two of you hanging out, but because, however much you may hate this, you *will* be judged by the company you keep. We wish we didn't have to tell you that, but again, we're not here to be nice. We're here to tell you how it is.

The importance of the company you choose to keep isn't just about a night out in a bar. Because in a bar, just like everywhere else, people are busy making assumptions about you every minute. In your everyday life, those assumptions can be based on where you work, or where you live, or where you're from, or a thousand other superficialities that seem irrelevant to who you are. In a bar, these things may matter, but they're not the overriding concerns a man will have when he first looks at you, when he first tries to figure out if you're someone he wants to approach. The first thing he's going to base his impression on is how you look and hold yourself. Are you shy? Sweet? Sassy? And the next thing he's going to base it on is how your friend acts. Is she a harpie? Hilarious? Fun to be around?

The most basic thing you need to think about is picking a friend who is going to flatter you. It doesn't have to be the same person every time—you want to hang out with a lot of different people, and hey, you may want to show off a different part of yourself on different occasions. But you'll want to size up how you're feeling on this particular night, think about what your agenda is, and then pick someone who is going to suit the mood. If you're feeling quiet, don't go out with someone who will never stop talking. If you're feeling gregarious, don't grab your quietest friend and hope she'll somehow survive while you're talking to someone else. Trust us—it never ends well.

That doesn't mean bad wingmen can't be good friends. They may be your *best* friends. But that doesn't mean they're your best choices for this particular evening.

Bad Wingmen

The Competitive Wingman

Believe us, there's enough competition among the women at the bar who *don't* know each other, all vying to get the attention of some poor sucker who is busy trying to get the score of the latest basketball game. You don't need the competition to come from your friend. Best-case scenario, you'll want to smack her. Worst-case scenario . . . well, let's just say we've seen the smack be more than just a fantasy. A good question to ask yourself: Is she your wingman, or are you hers?

We know two former college roommates who could not be better friends. While they've gone on to live apart, they're still on each other's speed dial, and when one of them gets into trouble, they're as close as sisters. They're great in a jam, but man, does it go bad in the bar. We don't even like them coming in together anymore, because the evening always dissolves into one of them talking horribly about the other to us while the other is in the bathroom.

Here's how it goes, and we mean every time: They come into the bar, looking to score. They're equally attractive and both hilarious, so they're on equal footing. Inevitably, a guy will come up and start talking to them. And just as inevitably, he'll pay more attention to one than the other, although it's anybody's guess that night who it will be. And then we can count the seconds until Bam! Cock block. It's just unbelievable—one of them will literally step in between the interested guy and her friend and turn so they can't talk without looking around her. Or the one who's feeling dissed will begin to talk too much, too loudly, always about herself. When it gets really bad, the one who is feeling dissed will start telling "funny" stories about her friend, and they almost always involve really bad interactions with men, followed by a derogatory laugh. The worst part? It always, always works. Those two manage to scare off any guy who gets close to them when they're out together, because neither allows a guy to get close to the other. It's absurd, because they both always go home alone, pissed at each other.

The Withdrawn Wingman

A few nights ago, we had two women come in. One was shy and the other more outgoing. There were a couple of guys at the bar, all fresh from work and dressed like it. The outgoing woman came up to us and asked us to send drinks over to the guys. The guys accepted the drinks and went over to the women and very politely said thank you, downed the drinks, and left. What had happened? The shy woman had panicked and immediately turned around, while the other woman expressed way too much eagerness, no doubt because she was trying to compensate for her shy friend. They were a bad balance: One woman came across as totally shut down, and the other as far too loud and out there. If they weren't standing together, especially in a bar, no doubt

Urban Myths About Alcohol

Repeat something often enough as "truth" and pretty soon it will just be assumed that it is the truth. But often, what people think about the things they're drinking is just plain wrong. Some examples:

"Grey Goose vodka won't give me a hangover" Despite the fancy advertising campaign, Grey Goose—as well as many "up-scale" alcohols out there—is just as potent as its less marketed neighbor in the liquor cabinet. No matter what you're drinking, drink enough of it and you'll still feel terrible the next day. That's because alcohol is a diuretic that binds with water in your blood and deprives you of hydration. The body responds by taking water wherever it can find it, one of those places being your brain. No wonder you have a headache!

"Gin makes me crazy" Well, maybe, but that's just because most gins are 94 proof (as compared to vodka's 80). If you're not used to drinking gin, of course it will wreak havoc on your system. Make sure to give it the respect it deserves, and you might come to love its magic flavor.

"If I drink energy drinks mixed with alcohol, I don't get as drunk" Sorry, kids. You might enjoy the buzz off the caffeine that's in something like Red Bull, but you're still going to be hurting from drinking too much alcohol.

"White wine has no calories" If you're on a diet, stick to diet sodas or waters. A glass of white wine has 80 calories, only five fewer than a glass of red wine.

they would have come across better. But having two guys approaching them in that setting brought out the worst in them. They would have been served better by going out for a quiet cocktail to catch up.

The Gay Wingman

That all-time favorite companion, your gay male best friend, may actually not be your best bet. Remember, when men are looking across the room at you, chances are they just see you with another guy. They're not spending the time to watch and listen in order to suss out that the two of you aren't sexually involved, and never would be. Also, you have to ask yourself, what kind of guy approaches a girl who is sitting with a guy? Actually, skip asking yourself—we'll answer that question for you. It's a guy who lacks respect for others and the normal boundaries that are so important in relationships.

Good Wingmen

The Supportive Wingman

This is the hardest person to find as a bar partner. Actually, this is the hardest kind of friend to find in life. Men are always jealous and a little in awe of the women who have this kind of friendship: They support each other no matter what, and they make each other look great. These are the friends who know how to generously tone it down when their friend is being hit on and happy about it; who know when to leave, and even more important, know when to stay. This friend is happy to give over the stage to you because you treat her with the same respect and consideration. She's confident enough that what is happening at that very moment is just about the moment and doesn't panic that she's not attractive if it's her friend who is getting the attention that night.

The Fabulosa Wingman

However weird this may be, one of the things we've noticed is that the most supportive friends, the ones who have the closest, most enduring friendships, are almost always equally attractive. Not that they both have the same hair color, but you can just tell they don't feel insecure physically around each other. In our experience, women tend to be much rougher about each other's looks than men ever would be, but it's clearly pretty crucial to women. And never, ever more crucial than in a bar.

The friends who always stop traffic are reflections of each

other. Your perfect fabulosa is a woman who is as pretty as you are. She's the person who always laughs hard—really hard—at your jokes, but makes you laugh just as hard at hers. And she's just as sharp as you are, too. One raise of an eyebrow to each other and you both get the message, whatever that message may be. The power of two, when it works, is always greater than the power of one.

The New Wingman

Sometimes, the best combinations we've seen are two women who come into a bar in the early stages of their friendship. We know it because they are almost flirting with each other, the way women seem to do when they're getting to know each other. They're engaged, inquisitive, and clearly enjoying each other's company.

Asking a new friend to go to a bar with you can be great because no matter how it goes, you're having a bonding experience together, something you can laugh at or gossip about the next day. Plus, something we've noticed is that new friends are always on their best behavior together. There's less cock blocking, less jostling for attention. Usually, these are the women who end up having the most fun on a night out, because they're in it together and don't take anything very seriously.

Never Wing Your Wingman

If you find yourself choosing (b) more than (a) for most of these, you might want to rethink your companion before your next night out.

1. **You leave a party. You want to:**

   a. Call her when you get home

   b. Not speak to her for a week

2. **When you ask her to join you, it's because:**

   a. She makes wherever you are more fun

   b. You feel obligated to include her in your fun

3. **When you're out together, you feel:**

   a. You're watching out for yourselves, while also keeping an eye on each other

   b. You need to keep an eye on her and what she's doing the whole time

4. **You're feeling great about something in your life. You:**

   a. Immediately call, knowing she'll want to celebrate you

   b. Instinctively edit yourself—it will just make her feel worse about herself

5. **You're talking to a guy you really like. You excuse yourself to go to the bathroom knowing:**

   a. She'll only make you look good

   b. They'll both be gone when you get back

Cocktail

What better way to toast the person who sticks by your side than with a **SIDECAR**? If you don't want to spring for cognac, any aged brandy will work. (Calvados, a French apple brandy, works beautifully.) You can make it with or without rimming the glass with sugar. For one drink, you'll need:

Slice of lemon

Sugar

1 ounce Courvoisier VS cognac

1 ounce Cointreau

¾ ounce fresh lemon juice

Orange twist

Wet the rim of a cocktail glass with a slice of lemon, then dip the rim into a dish of sugar. Shake off the excess sugar and place the glass in the freezer. Pour the cognac, Cointreau, and lemon juice into a cocktail shaker; add ice and shake vigorously. Strain into the chilled glass and garnish with a twist.

Dressing for Success Doesn't Mean Dressing in Less

We know, from what we hear from our female customers, that there is no aspect of the night that you think about more than what you're going to wear. That's why we're amazed that maybe only 25 percent of the women we see at our bar actually get it right—and that's being generous.

Amazed because hey, you are *clearly* the smarter sex, so how is it possible that when you are actually thinking it through you get it so wrong, so often? The trick to dressing well is unbelievably simple. Ready?

Because this is something your friends will never tell you. There are some things, maybe many things, that just aren't flattering. Period. On the other hand, there is no single woman on this planet who can't make herself look better than she does in her pajamas if she just figures out a few simple rules. So put down that *Glamour* magazine, and take it from us. Here are the golden rules, the Dos and Don'ts, of how to be comfortable with yourself and please most guys.

Don't Worry About *Vogue*-ing

The first rule: No matter what your friends say, no matter what magazines say, you have to dress so that you're comfortable. If it's important to you and you feel better about yourself because you're dressed in trendy clothing, knock yourself out. But believe us— few men are going to pick up, in a quick scan, whether you're wearing jeans or corduroys, or that those bell-bottoms are from last season. But they *are* going to know, in that moment that decides whether their eyes linger or move on, if you're feeling confident.

The easiest way to do this is to have two or three

road-tested outfits that you know make you feel powerful and cool. That way, even if you're in a hurry while
you're trying to get out the door, you know there are a
couple of things that look great on you, whether it's
the perfect pair of jeans that make you feel thin on a
fat day or the low-cut top that shows off your cleavage
when you're having a confident day.

We promise you that unlike women, men will
never, ever call each other the next day and ask of the
previous evening's conquest, "So, what was she wearing?" After all, it's all about getting you out of those
clothes as soon as possible!

Men Don't Equate the Vastness of Your Emotional Life with the Depth of Your Cleavage

Men take something like two seconds to form an impression of someone, so really give thought to what
you're wearing. If you want to wear that really short
skirt and really low-cut shirt, that's totally fine (you
won't notice men complaining!), but you should antic-
ipate that you're going to get attention paid to your
legs and your bustline before anything else. Every-

thing is a consequence of your choices, and the sooner you realize that, the more powerful you'll feel.

Look, we love a sexy customer more than any other kind. We like looking at her, the other men in the bar like looking at her, and that means there are very happy men behind the bar and in front of it. But there are ways to look sexy, to feel sexy, without overplaying it so it's the only thing men see, and become incapable of seeing past it.

What's sexier than a naked woman? A woman in lingerie. Men love a little left to the imagination. They always, *always* prefer to see a woman in her underwear rather than naked, at least when it comes to sexual fantasies. It's about fanning desire.

If you are determined to get laid that night, that's cool, but if you're one of those women who turns around upset the morning after, time and time again, wondering why they don't call you back when they seemed so crazy about you, take a look at your outfit and see if maybe you aren't overplaying your hand just a touch. If you're in doubt, *please* don't ask your best girlfriend: While her best attribute may be that she's not a guy, she's *not a guy*. Instead, ask a guy friend and tell him you need the truth.

And one final point we can't emphasize enough: Heels can be very, very sexy. But if when you're walking in them you look like you should be playing for a professional football team—legs splayed and toes clinging to the earth like you're about to be tackled— even the most expensive shoes can turn into your worst accessory. How do you know? Walk in front of a mirror. If your ankles are wobbling, or you feel unsteady— and this is while you're sober, mind you—think about how miserable feeling and looking you'll be by the end of the night. While it may fulfill some rescue fantasy of yours when he takes you to the emergency room with a sprained ankle, trust us, unlike you, he won't think it's a bonding experience.

Dressing Appropriately Isn't Just for the Workplace

You might look absolutely fantastic in your long black evening gown, but you're going to look pretty frickin' strange at your local bar, unless you're prepared to make up some long-winded story about where you've come from (and if you haven't figured this out already, men are all for mystery, but lying is exhausting for you and usually wasted on them). Nor should you stumble into a more upscale place in your sweatpants with "Juicy" written across the butt (a trend that most men find totally confusing, by the way; as ignorant as men may be on many subjects, they don't actually need *that* spelled out for them).

You no doubt put a lot of thought into what you're going to wear to work in the morning, about what will be both appropriate and impressive. Do exactly the same thing for an evening out. Again, what works in the world works in a bar, and vice versa. And it's a hell of a lot easier to learn to dress for a glass of wine than for a meeting.

Now for the advanced level: You don't just want to make sure you're comfortable where you are going. What too few of our customers give thought to, even if they've nailed the perfect outfit, is the physical logistics of being in a bar. If you're planning on spending the night on a barstool, remember that once you hop up, a short skirt will ride up at least a few inches, and low-rider jeans go the other way. We're not saying you should or shouldn't have your thong hanging out (hey, men kinda like it, even if they shouldn't), but we *are* saying you should be aware of it. And spending the whole night pulling down your skirt or tucking in your underwear is just going to distract you from what you're actually there for.

People are drawn to comfortable, confident people because those qualities are contagious, and men like being around such women because it allows *them* to be more comfortable. Not to mention that if you're comfortable and not worrying about how you look, you have all the more energy to focus your attention on them!

Remember: You're Not a Psychic

Once you get to know a guy you'll learn about his personal preferences, but don't even think about it before you open that door and walk on in. As one buddy says, "Everyone has a type, and even I don't know why I like what I like. It's cute but not beautiful . . . I don't know. It's weird because not all the girls I date are the same, but there's a certain look and style that catches my eye, and I can't say what exactly it is that's so alluring about them."

That's again why it's totally important to be cool with how you look, because it's absolutely impossible to dress for a man, especially a man you have never met. We know you won't believe us, but it's women's magazines and the society we live in that is your enemy, not men. Men don't notice those "love handles." They have no idea why you obsess over the extra five pounds, which they only think make you more luscious. And if he is one of those men who likes to date models, and only models, what are you doing? You can't, and shouldn't, compete. Unless you also happen to be a model, it's not going to happen, and you run the risk of the predictable rejection.

Sure, we men all have our own particular tastes about what turns us on, but we promise, it doesn't hinge on anything that nuanced. In any case, you're not going to be able to read his mind in terms of what his type is, so it's crucial to feel as at home in your body as you can. For instance, one of us (we're not saying who) thinks tattoos on women are about as sexy as they get. The other of us thinks they're tacky. If you tried to guess what a guy likes before you even talk to him, you're going to spend a lot of time obsessing and very little time actually talking. And if you've attracted a guy because you've dressed in a way that's totally out of character, that's not fair to either of you if you both decide to see each other again. Be true to the person you are, to the person he might meet the next morning over brunch, when you haven't had time to raid your girlfriend's closet, or applied tons of eyeliner that you'll never wear again.

What a guy notices is that a woman respects herself, that she's comfortable with herself. And you really, really can't ask anyone else—especially a man—to respect you if you don't respect yourself.

You Can Never Go Wrong Underplaying It

One of our good friends is this beautiful woman from the South, where expressing femininity is an art form. This woman spends about forty minutes a day putting on her makeup, and we swear to you there is no way to tell she is wearing any—that's part of the art of what she's doing.

She stands out to us because she's so hugely in the minority. Men may have no idea what goes into the subtle effects of being a hot woman, nor do we have any interest in the topic, but there's something scary about a woman who slathers it on. On a deeper level, it's probably because it makes men mistrustful: What are you trying to hide? But on a much more superficial level, it's just not attractive. Red lipstick? Love it. Mascara? Ditto. But chances are that more than that and we wonder why you're dressed up for Halloween, even though it's May.

And while we're at it, *please* don't douse yourself in perfume. You can never underestimate the power of smell, which is the most powerful of the senses, and the one most tied into memory We love the way women smell as much as the next guy, but men want to think it's for them only. Wear enough to draw him in, not to repel him. Men want to smell it when they bend in close to talk to you, or give you a hug or a kiss. If you give guys a headache before they've gotten within a foot of you, you're not about to be closing the distance.

A Clothes Call

Back to our favorite study group: the men and women who hang out at our bar. We pointed out various women and asked guys to comment on what she was wearing. OK, so we had to bribe the guys with free drinks, but they did oblige us.

We pointed to: A woman wearing worn-in Levi's and a button-down shirt.

He said: "She looks totally hot. I like that she doesn't look like she overthought what she's wearing. Plus, there's nothing sexier to me than a button-down shirt. It makes me think about how she would look wearing mine after we've gone to bed."

We pointed to: A woman wearing a tight halter top, short skirt, and killer heels.

He said: "I'm certainly not going to think that she's wife material—no way am I introducing a woman who dresses like that to my mother—but she's definitely got my attention. Whether she'll keep it past tonight? Doubtful."

We pointed to: A woman wearing a tube top, jeans, and high heels.

He said: "Love that. She's showing off her chest, and yes, I'm noticing, but the jeans make it seem like she didn't put hours into primping herself. I look at her and think, 'low maintenance and sexy.'"

We pointed to: A woman sitting at the bar with her thong hanging out of her low-rise pants.

He said: "I know it's wrong, but I love that. It's like she doesn't know what's happening, and she's just accidentally giving me a peek at what's underneath. I can't help but want to see more."

We pointed to: A woman in a turtleneck, cardigan sweater, and khakis.

He said: "Wow. When I first looked over, I looked right past her. I feel like she's wearing so many layers I can only imagine how much work it would be to take them off. But she looks like she's having a lot of fun, so maybe I'm wrong. If she takes off her cardigan, I'll take it as a sign and go right up."

Cocktail

If you like accessorizing, you'll love a **PIMM'S CUP**, which you can dress up with any number of garnishes. It's also a snap to make, as easy as slipping into your favorite pair of jeans. For one drink, you'll need:

1½ ounces Pimm's No. 1

½ ounce Cointreau

½ ounce fresh lime juice

Sprig of mint

3 cucumber slices

Seasonal fruit

Ginger ale

Pour the Pimm's, Cointreau, and lime juice over ice in a tall glass. Garnish with mint, cucumber, and fruit. Shake or stir briefly. Top off with ginger ale.

Your Destination Informs Your Destiny

All of the time and energy you've put into thinking about who you are and what you want, all of
the thought you've given about how to present yourself
so you look your best, can end up as an exercise in futil-
ity if you don't give extra weight to another crucial
consideration: Where are you going to go, and how are
you going to act once you get there?

Your ball gown will be strange, not stunning, if you
decide to head for six o'clock happy hour at your local
beer hall. And all the confidence you feel in your sexiest jeans will evaporate if you walk into a swanky hotel

bar where people are dressed in suits. So first, you have to match your mood and your outfit and your desires with the place you're going to go.

Then you have to think about how you're going to use that place to your advantage. And we mean the actual *space* of that room. Because once you choose your destination, then you have an opportunity to make the most of it, whether that is positioning yourself so that as many people as possible will see you reflected in the mirrors, or staying out of the dark corners where no one can see you.

Picking a Place

Choosing a place to go can be a difficult decision. Again you must decide based on what it is you are looking for. From the brightly lit restaurant bar to the dark bustling club, there are serious differences in how these spaces affect the customers, and what the customers are there looking for. The elements that infuse a specific place with its own vibe and energy break down into pretty simple categories.

LIGHTING Dim, warm lighting makes *everyone*

look better. Because this kind of lighting creates a feeling of cozy intimacy, people tend to be more open. In other words, hookups happen left and right. One of the ironies about dim lighting is that because people tend to be more unguarded and relaxed, the energy level is usually higher than in a place that's brightly lit, even if that place is more "cheerful."

MUSIC Music is a big indication of what a place has to offer, since most bars make very conscious decisions about what they put on the turntable in order to please their regulars. A bar that is playing light jazz will be more sultry, inviting customers to linger over cocktails and offering the opportunity for subtle flirtation, while a place that is playing hip-hop or something with a stronger beat will make people more uninhibited and unconsciously inform them that it's OK to do everything faster, from drinking to hooking up.

Making Yourself Shine

Once you've chosen the place you want to go, then it's time to think about how you can use that place to make you shine. All the tools are in front of you, but most

Alcohol Really Is a Cure-all, and Other Wisdom from the Bar

Many of the spirits, tonics, and bitters that we drink were created and used for medicinal purposes. As time passed, bartenders' understanding of alcohol's many uses evolved, which goes far beyond just making the customer feel better. Some good tips bartenders have passed down through the ages:

Did you spill red wine on yourself? Believe it or not, white wine gets out red wine stains. It works so well that just by rubbing the stain with the white wine, it will become barely noticeable.

Do you have the hiccups? Don't hold your breath. Instead, try this, which works nine out of ten times: Dowse a lemon wedge in Angostura bitters and dip it in sugar. Bite down on the lemon and suck out the juice. The bitters are key because they help settle your stomach as well as get rid of the hiccups.

Are you getting drunk? One of our fellow bartenders told us his father's secret to fighting off the bed spins—he would do a shot of olive oil whenever he felt that he'd had too much to drink. The olive oil coats the stomach and helps slow down the absorption of the alcohol.

Did you scrape yourself? Pour a bit of vodka on a napkin and press it to your wound in order to sterilize it. Vodka's your best bet because the high alcohol content kills any germs and helps avoid infection.

Do you have a stomachache? Again, bitters to the rescue! Try an Italian Amaro or a shot of Fernet-Branca. The more bitter the better. Remember, medicine isn't supposed to go down easy.

Are you having terrible cramps? Try a shot of Polish blackberry brandy. A waitress we worked with told us this did the trick for her, and soon it caught on with the rest of the female staff, all of whom swore it worked for them, as well.

Are you hung over? There are so many cures out there to take the edge off the price of your fun night out, but we think the most reliable antidotes are also the oldest: vitamin C, vitamin B, Gatorade, aspirin, water, and, of course, time to sleep it off.

people don't know they're just sitting there waiting to be taken advantage of!

STOOLS Literally, a chance to be put on a pedestal—how can you turn that down? By sitting on a bar stool, you are raised above eye level, which immediately gives you a chance of being noticed over those who are standing. For women who are uncomfortable with their height, this can be a great equalizer. More important, it will immediately make you more comfortable physically because you're not spending the energy that's necessary to stand (let alone balance a drink and not get knocked over by the rest of the crowd).

THE STANDING ROOM IN FRONT OF A BAR Even if you can't get a stool, you can still use the bar space to your advantage. First of all, if you can easily get to the bar and order a drink, you can ask the bartender to tell you who's vacating a stool soon—since we're pouring their drinks and giving them their bills, we know who's about to head out. Second, standing can be a good way to interact with people, because you have mobility you don't have when you're sitting. One good trick at a crowded bar is to go up behind a group of guys and ask them to get a drink for you. Even if they don't buy it for you, they may get our attention faster simply because they're taller than you are, and you will have a few minutes to check them out.

THE CURVE OF A BAR Forgive us for speaking about a bar the way some men speak about women, but we are passionate about them—bars, we mean; and women— the curvier the better. The curvier the bar, the easier to see the other customers. The more easily you can see other people, the more possibilities are, er, laid out for you. And more important, the more easily you will be seen by other people. Plus, it's a hell of a lot less claustrophobic than finding yourself backed into a bar where you can only see to either side and there are twelve people waiting behind you. Sit facing the bar, angled slightly toward your wingman so your profile is still visible to the people standing behind you.

MIRRORS Restaurants, bars, and clubs purposely place mirrors to help create a larger sense of space. But they are also in places that allow you to see more people, and allow more people to see you. Instead of staring at your reflection, use the mirrors as a way to scope out the rest of the bar. You can rule out a lot of duds that way without having to establish eye contact, let alone talk to them.

BATHROOM LINES OK, this is going to sound strange,

but we can't tell you the number of connections we've seen made while people wait in common areas to use the bathroom. The rules of engagement are less serious with neither party on home turf, or committing to a drink. Plus, you might as well try to find something positive in everything, including long bathroom lines!

TIMING It's important to think about when you're showing up, since every bar's atmosphere changes as the night goes on. For example, from five to seven PM tends to be an after-work crowd, and from seven to, let's say, ten PM, is when people tend to order up some food with whoever they're with. This means that the best time to meet someone, when people are starting to look around, tends to be later at night, when people aren't sticking with their own parties. They've caught up with their work crowd, and they've finished dinner. Ideally, try to get to the bar just a little bit before dinnertime is over, because you can claim real estate at the bar and have a good view of the customers as they come in.

What's Your Perfect Setting?

For every possible occasion there's a perfect place to be. Here's a quick guide that will never fail:

1. If you've been fired, head to a pub for darts and beer.
2. If you've gotten a promotion, go to the fanciest place you can find and order a glass of champagne.
3. If you've been dumped, get to a sports bar, STAT, and remember how many men there are in the world.
4. If you're feeling rowdy, go to a place with music so you can dance off the energy.
5. If you need to talk about an "issue," find a seat at the bar of a nice, quiet restaurant.
6. If you need to drink and then crash, stop by your favorite neighborhood bar where you can get service quickly and get out of there even faster.
7. If you need to feel pretty, go to a bar that's a bit more downscale so you can feel secure.
8. If you're feeling pretty, go to the hip bar of the moment to show yourself off.
9. If you want to drink by yourself, take the best company you know to a table for one at an elegant hotel bar, where they're accustomed to travelers coming through solo.
10. If your pet died, take yourself to bed. And only to bed.

Cocktail

One of our favorite places is the New York speakeasy Jack and Charlie's, now known as the 21 Club. Jack and Charlie's originated the famous **SOUTH SIDE** cocktail in the 1920s. We've substituted citrus-flavored vodka for the gin called for in the original recipe; the light, minty taste is great in the summer. For one drink, you'll need:

1¼ ounces Stoli Citrus vodka

1 ounce fresh lemon juice

½ ounce simple syrup (see page 16)

Sprig of mint

Splash of club soda

Place a cocktail glass in the freezer. Combine all the ingredients except the club soda in a cocktail shaker; add ice and shake vigorously. Add the club soda and strain into the chilled glass.

They're Called "Dream" Men for a Reason

Once you figure out what kind of woman you are, it's time to take a look at another reality: the truth about who men really are. And trust us, however pathetic it may be, you haven't been *entirely* wrong all those years you complained to your girlfriends that men are basically nitwits and morons who could have used some more years being raised by their mamas. But here are the two things men feel women miss about them all the time, the two inherent truths about them: 1. They're incredibly insecure (they just fake it better than you do). 2. They are programmed for sex.

We'll repeat number two one more time because

it's so, so crucial for you to understand this as an adult woman in sexual relationships. Yes, men are here to woo you, but they're here to woo you for one reason only. Sex!!!!! Kind of takes your breath away, right? But the thing is, at the end of the day, that's what it's all about. Well, maybe not the end of the day, but the end of the night. At least at the end of a night in a bar.

But now we offer up the panacea for the problem, by divulging a secret most men hope you'll never learn: You have much more power than you think you do. In fact, for a good part of the mating dance you have *all* the power. Because the first question that enters a man's mind when he meets you is, "Can I?" And the first thing that occurs to you is "Would I?" Right there, you've got the power imbalance starting. And believe us, men are going to do everything they can to right it.

The thing is, men are programmed to be the keepers of romance, simply because you are programmed to be the keepers of sex. That means that while men might not be hardwired to deliver the roses, or give the compliments, or whisper sweet nothings, they will because that's what's required of them. That's what they are going to have to give up, in order to get you to give something up, too. Romance for sex. It's that simple.

Very few men admit this. It's not sexy, and it goes against the very thing they're trying to do, which is to woo you with romance. But you're the person who is going to make the decision about what happens as a result of those gestures, the person who is going to say yes or no in response to his actions. Which means you've gotten the upper hand. And this is where it gets to be fun, because you now have an inkling about how much power you have. That's the moment when you get to decide what you want from them.

But first, you need to decide what kind of guy is interesting to you at the moment. And trust us, there aren't so many different kinds in a bar. That doesn't mean that men aren't multidimensional and worth your time. We're just saying that as often as we see women make great first impressions, we're usually seeing at least three guys making terrible ones. And the impressions aren't not necessarily wrong. Because you shouldn't be *looking* for love in a bar. You should be looking for fun, and for the experience of feeling more confident about yourself. So here we go. For better or worse, still, you gotta love 'em . . .

Mr. Perfect

Mr. Perfect is the person who's off saving the world when he's not making sure everyone has a drink and enough to eat. He is effortlessly handsome and charismatic and somehow pays the bills while doing good in the world. When old ladies need someone to walk them across the street, that's when Mr. Perfect materializes.

HOW TO SPOT HIM If it looks too good to be true, it is. Always. Love is not a fairy tale—that's why romance novels exist. If you pay attention, the perfect guy is always the one where *everything* is about him. The sneaky thing in here is this: Mr. Perfect makes you think that it's about you—and you miss that pleasing you is really just about making himself feel good about . . . himself.

We see that guy all the time—in fact, we just saw one the other night. A couple sits down at the bar for dinner; she's dressed to the nines, diamonds, pearls, the whole deal. Her date is, no surprise, master of the universe. He has impeccable manners, holding the seat out for her, acting attentive, ordering the best wine. You get the idea. He engages the woman in conversation, he pretends to be paying attention to her, but we can tell he isn't listening. How? Because there are no followup questions. Everything about his manner is perfect—and he is, we're sure, a nice guy—but he's not interested in anything but his *own* perfection.

WHERE TO SPOT HIM Five-star hotel or established upscale bar.

PROS You will be filled with pride in public when you're with Mr. Perfect. (And the old ladies he's walking across the street will remind you that you should be, in case you forget.) Your friends will swoon with envy as he buys you drinks, walks you home, remembers your birthday (and theirs), and knows his way around a wine list with impressive ease.

CONS How many times have you whined to your girlfriends, "But he's perfect, what's wrong with me?" Well, we're here to tell you something. The "nice" guy may be your perfect date at weddings and family functions, but he also may be the first person to leave you cold in life (and maybe even bed). He's the guy who will go down on you for hours ... and end up being impotent. Trust us: If you can find a man who you will really love and really lust after, you've hit gold. But if you're looking for "perfect," chances are you're going to end up feeling pretty lonely, and worse, when you try to tell your friends about what exactly it is that isn't fulfilling you, you're going to be left struggling for examples and feeling even more foolish. (After all, they're perfect!)

We're not saying "Mr. Perfect" isn't going to be a nice guy. But "polished" and "charming" is always going to rank the highest. Because in his mind, life is still a popularity contest, and he's waiting for the "Most Popular" prize. Mr. Perfect is the one your family is going to like more than you do. Mr. Perfect is going to leave you feeling lonely. Insecure. So much *less* than perfect.

The Empty Charmer, aka The Pussy Hound

This is the guy who nailed down his act as a high school football star practicing on the whole squad of cheerleaders. This many years later, he's got the act down cold.

HOW TO SPOT HIM He's handsome, he's charming. Man, is he charming . . .

WHERE TO SPOT HIM At clubs or the hot places that are packed, where the sexual energy is charged to the max.

PROS Did we mention the charm? This is the guy

who sends women off to the bathroom with their girl-friends to squeal with delight and say, "You're never going to believe what he said!"

CONS We believe it, because we hear it all the time. The empty charmer has only so many tricks, most of which are made unnecessary by the first one: beautiful eyes that he uses for incredible and fixed eye contact. It's amazing, because while women can be the most compli-cated creatures in the world, we have never seen that one simple trick fail: a guy wants to bring a woman to her knees—or his bed—he just has to blink his long eye-lashes to make a woman feel like the only woman he's ever seen before. But the thing is, the empty charmer is in it for one thing, and one thing only, and that's getting laid for the night, or for the next month if he's bored. He's the one who will make you the saddest, because he'll never give you anything to dislike about him to comfort yourself with when he leaves. Which he will.

The Number-Hunter

This guy is very similar to the pussy hound but he lacks balls. He'll always approach women because he knows he'll never have to follow up. He's interested in the quantity of numbers he can get, rather than the quality. And last, but most important, he's influential among or easily influenced by his friends.

HOW TO SPOT HIM   He interacts with many women for short periods of time but does it very intensely (after all, he's got to get a number when he's done with the conversation!). If you see someone moving through women as if he's enjoying a quick but rich meal—appetizer, main course, dessert—you've found him.

WHERE TO SPOT HIM   Everywhere.

PROS   You can flirt for free.

CONS   You can get confused and think he's going to call.

The Emotionally Hurt Hipster

He's living with his sister until he figures out how to sell his poetry. He tells you he's learned to play the guitar at night. He's depressed. So depressed. But instead of thinking "the dude can't pay his rent," you hear violins (or guitar strings). Like the other guys we've told you about before, he's probably really nice. A good guy. Solid friends, pays his taxes, nothing dangerous.

HOW TO SPOT HIM The puppy dog eyes, the wad of singles crumpled up in his pocket that he counts out slowly as he's paying for his drink, knowing these are his last.

WHERE TO SPOT HIM Dive bars, hip places.

PROS He's disarmingly honest. You don't have to worry about being played by him—he's the guy who, if you said "I just want to be friends," would jump at the chance and bring you chicken soup when you're sick. Dates will be interesting, if only because he's endlessly open about what he's been through, and while you're nodding with empathy, he, unlike the pussy hound, isn't thinking, "Yeah! I got her to bed with that one!" Plus, he'll go to chick flicks with you and cry even harder than you do.

CONS He may never get it together. Reread that sentence. By the age of, let's say, twenty-seven, a man is hopefully on a certain path of what he intends to be. We're not saying they can't have failures or bumps, but a man isn't so dumb that he can't "soul search" while managing to pay the bills, even if it's by holding down a gig he's not passionate about.

If you have a lot of energy, no reason this guy isn't for you, but just understand you will always be paying the health insurance and picking up every tab. It's absolutely crucial not to confuse two points: 1. What someone does for a living is not who they are. 2. If they can't get it together with *some* kind of job, chances are they can't get it together outside of that job, either. People who have it together have it together across the board.

Peter Pan

Peter Pan is the guy who tries to make you laugh by immediately telling you a joke—and it's always a good one. Such a good one that beer comes out of your nose, which makes him flush with pleasure. Unlike Mr. Perfect, he truly gets joy in seeing you feel joy, not just as a reflection of himself. Peter Pan is like a golden retriever puppy: warm, furry, friendly, beloved by all.

HOW TO SPOT HIM One of our favorite customers is a Peter Pan, because at the end of the night of pouring martinis for people with attitudes, it's really cool to hand him a beer and watch him open it with the bottle opener on his key chain. Hey—less work for us, and he's totally chill, but the dude is thirty-five years old. And he's still quoting *South Park*. Makes us laugh, but . . .

WHERE TO SPOT HIM Neighborhood bars, where he's dropping by to say hi to friends.

PROS Peter Pan is probably the most fun guy you could possibly hook up with. He's funny, he's got great friends, he's legitimately enthusiastic. He's got all the energy of a fifteen-year-old, seemingly untempered by life's experiences. And he plays along with whatever it is he knows so many women say are the most attractive qualities in men.

He'll be completely psyched to come join you and your friends for a drink, but also just as delighted when you want a night with the girls—Peter Pan is sure of his ability to have fun no matter the situation and doesn't need you to make it for him. He's honest, but he's not egregiously earnest. He'll always make you laugh, because he's kind and he's silly.

CONS Kind and silly are positive attributes for four-year-olds and house pets. (We're not saying they're not necessary characteristics, but they should be part of the mix, not the whole deal.) And like a golden retriever puppy, he's probably not housebroken. Mr. Perfect will never leave the seat up. Peter Pan will not only leave the seat up, he'll also pee on the rim and then shrug and giggle when you call him on it. And while he'll be a great date for your college roommate's Sunday brunch, the chances that he remembers where he's supposed to be and when he's supposed to be there are nil.

A Drinker Defined

We're all for *not* judging a book by its cover, but we have to admit there's a lot you can tell about a guy from his drink order. Chances are good that if he . . .

1. Drinks martinis: He's mature and comfortable with himself.

2. Drinks margaritas (and it's not summer): He's a closet frat boy who wishes he worked at Club Med.

3. Drinks single malt scotch: He's an intellectual, although perhaps a bit pretentious.

4. Drinks champagne: He's out to impress, or he's celebrating something.

5. Drinks cosmopolitans: He might be a better personal shopper than a date.

6. Drinks beer: He's a regular guy not out to get hammered (assuming it's not from a funnel).

7. Drinks tequila shots: He's more interested in getting fucked up than he is in you.

8. Drinks something with chocolate in it: He belongs in Weight Watchers. Or will soon.

9. Drinks club soda with lime: He's sober.

10. Drinks water: He's broke.

Cocktail

No eye-opening cocktail is more famous than the **BLOODY MARY**, one of the few alcoholic beverages acceptable to drink before the sun goes down. The two main ingredients are tomato juice and vodka, but you can play around with various spices to make a Bloody Mary that suits you perfectly. For one drink, you'll need:

2 ounces Level vodka

Tomato juice (at least 2 ounces, if not more)

Celery salt

Fresh-ground black pepper

Tabasco sauce

Grated horseradish

Worcestershire sauce (preferably Lea & Perrins)

Lemon wedges (garnish)

Celery stalks (garnish)

Pickled vegetables (garnish)

If you're making drinks for a crowd, lay out all the ingredients on a table or bar and let your friends make their own perfect eye-openers. Combine the ingredients and garnish with lemon wedges, celery, and vegetables.

Being Fluent in Body Language Can Ease Your Journey

OK, darlin', it's time for your closeup. You're hanging out in the bar, breathing a sigh of relief that you've made it this far and finally relaxing and having a good time. But don't forget this is the first part of the night, when the personal decisions you have made up until now begin playing out in public.

What's the public going to see? What is it, exactly, that you are communicating across the room to anyone who might catch a glimpse of you? Granted, thinking about your body language doesn't seem as sexy or interesting as figuring out which pair of jeans is the most flattering, but trust us, how you present yourself in a bar is far more important than whatever nonsense you have going on in your head about your fat jeans vs. your thin jeans. An ordinary-looking woman can become completely captivating if she's animated, while a runway model can look like a total dolt if she just sits there with a blank expression. Remember, these are guys looking at you, and they're making their instant impressions. A raised eyebrow, a wide smile—these can create impressions that a perfectly fitting (or not) pair of jeans won't have a chance to.

If you can master these finer points of using your body to allure, you will be able to slay men. And you *can*, with the beauty your very own body has to offer, however much you might not believe it. You can learn to feel more powerful. Plus, you can save a lot of energy: Knowing how to physically communicate certain parts of your personality will take a hell of a lot less energy than trying to hold a conversation across a deafening bar.

Keep Yourself Open

We mean that literally. If you can help it, no matter how uncomfortable you are, don't fold yourself up like a piece of origami. It registers to men that you don't want to talk to anybody, or that the man who might be interested in you is going to have to unpretzel you in more ways than one. Keep your hands in your lap so you make sure not to cross your arms across your chest (which, in any case, hides your breasts, two of your features men covet the most, regardless of their size). If you feel yourself slouching, try simply shifting your weight forward off your tailbone and onto the back of your thighs, which will automatically make you sit up straighter. (OK, OK, so one of our women friends taught us this trick. But it's a good one, right? Check it out.)

If you're perched on a bar stool and it's too uncomfortable to lean forward off your tailbone, go ahead and turn a bit to the side, put one foot up on the rung of the stool beside you, and rest your elbow on the bar or the next chair. You'll find that you've fully opened your body but look totally casual. If there's no back, cross your legs and raise them a bit so your knees are pressed up against the bar, and then hold the top one

between your hands. It'll give you a little more support, but you still look approachable and laid back. By
sitting up straight, you just look so much more inviting. Plus, you'll be able to catch our eye when you want
a drink!

Feel Free to Gesture

Here's one time we're going to tell you to avoid your
mother or grandmother's advice, should they have
suggested that you not use your hands in conversation.
We think gesturing is super sexy. Most men do. It's
lyrical, and it adds rhythm to what you're saying, like
the perfect bass note in a jazz trio. Your gestures should
be much less studied than your posture, because studied gestures will look just that—studied. But things
like running your fingers through your hair, or slap-
ping your thigh when something makes you laugh—
these things convey intimate details about who you
are, and men feel like you're being yourself when you
relax and literally and physically act like yourself. As
with all things, don't overdo any of 'em, since that can
lead to looking like you have nervous tics more than

endearing personality traits, but here are some of the things you might do that our male customers confessed to having a weakness for:

- Running your fingers through your hair or tucking it behind your ears.
- Stroking your neck—men automatically imagine that they're the ones who get to do that to you next.
- Using your hands to tell a story. Women who use their hands when they speak? We love 'em. Our customers love 'em. And it can be a quick attention-getter. Remember that men are attracted by anything that moves. Be the thing that moves, and he'll keep his eye on you. Add an occasional quick, light touch on our leg or arm when you're trying to make a point, and men are goners. You want to be as flirtatious with your hands and your body as you are with your words. (One caveat: Until you know a man, don't touch him on his head or his face. Remember how you say men are like dogs? Make that stray dogs. Go at them too quickly, touch them in a vulnerable place, or take them by surprise and they'll either snap or go running into the corner with their tail between their legs.)

Five Ways to Get a Bartender's Attention and Keep It

1. Catch his eye—a bartender is always looking up to see who needs what—and then gesture. Don't yell.

2. Know what you want to drink before the bartender asks. If you're ordering for other people, also know what they want.

3. If you're ordering for other people, please have everyone's money in hand, ready to pay, so the bartender doesn't have to wait.

4. If you want a specific brand, ask for it by name. Also, give the spirit name first. "Cranberry vodka" is different from "Vodka cranberry."

5. If you know you'll be coming back for another round and you're paying with a credit card, leave the tab open so the bartender doesn't have to run through new charges when you return.

Try Not to Fidget

Remember, the entire point of everything we're telling you is to try to get you to wrap your head around a single truth: There is nothing sexier than—or more important than—your comfort level. Think about the sexiest women you know. Don't they all radiate a natural comfort and harmony with their environment? Well, nothing undoes the impression of confidence and security like fidgeting.

Fidgeting is *not* to be confused with gesturing. Gestures are your personal signatures. Gestures are deeply individual, the exclamation point at the end of a sentence. They are the movements that communicate, nonverbally, "Look at me! Pay attention to what I'm saying!" Fidgeting, however, is a universal manifestation of anxiety, jerky movements that add a question mark to everything that comes out of your mouth. Fidgeting is tapping your foot, drumming your fingers, crossing-uncrossing-crossing your legs every thirty seconds. Fidgeting is abrupt, it's annoying, and it breaks the natural rhythm of any conversation or growing intimacy. Obviously don't be a statue, but don't act like an extra in *Rain Man*.

Keep Your Distance . . . But Not Too Much

There's no hard-and-fast rule to this except the signals you're getting from the person across from you. If he's leaning back, don't lean in. If he's taken a step back, don't close the distance. This is one of the few places where you should absolutely follow a man's lead. Men are more physical creatures than women when it comes to going out and punching each other in a boxing ring or tackling each other on a football field, and yet they are much more uncomfortable with close physical intimacy. Think about it—how often do you see best male friends hugging? And when they do, unless they're European, it's usually quick and punctuated with a playful punch or slap on the back. You want to be open, you want to be accessible, but when it comes to the physical dance of flirtation, *always let the man set the tone.*

Close the Gap

This is so friggin' hard that if you can master it, you'll be in the AP class of flirts. In fact, you could teach the class. Here's what we're talking about: You're in a crowded, loud bar. It's your job to get him not to look at the woman behind you, or the TV on the wall, or, God forbid, his watch.

One of our favorite tricks was taught to us by an old friend. When she gets into a conversation with a man she likes, she begins to back up, so slowly it is imperceptible (except to us, now that we know!). Without realizing it, the man almost always follows her lead by stepping forward as she begins to step back, and within five minutes, she's got her back up against the wall, which does two things: She's more comfortable (as we said, standing against a wall will give you support), but she's also drawn him out of the mayhem and into a world she's created, a virtual intimacy where the fact that she's still in a crowded bar suddenly seems irrelevant. Basically, it's sensory deprivation. He can't see the bartender, he can't see the clock, he can't see anyone else in the room—literally—because she's standing against a blank wall and he's facing her. But her coup de grâce? Once she's got him facing her in the corner, she lowers her voice, drawing him in even closer. She knows that men need to be the ones who *think* they're initiating physical intimacy or closeness, but she's engineered it so it has not only happened, she's made him think he did it himself.

How to Make Your Approach

When we started asking around about whether guys like to get approached or do the approaching, we thought we'd be getting a mixed bag of answers. Instead, the answers tended to be the same: Almost every guy said he'd love it if a woman approached him but it almost never happened. Here are some ways they said they'd be comfortable—and turned on—having a woman come up to them:

- "Something that would immediately put me at ease would be if a woman pretended there was some other guy annoying her or giving her strange looks, and asked me if she could stand and talk to me in order to get rid of him. It would make me feel like she thought I was a good protector, as well as that she wanted to talk to me."

- "I'd love it if a woman was direct. I think that would be really hot. If a woman came over and said, 'I saw you standing there and I just have to tell you, I think you're really attractive,' that would be awesome."

- "Know about sports. But really."
- "Compliment me on what I'm wearing. Say, 'I like your shirt,' or 'cool tie.' We know you know about clothes, so if you like what I'm wearing, I've already done something right."
- "All a woman would have to do is smile at me and say hello. That would do the trick!"

Cocktail

We love the idea of working with what you have—especially when it comes to drinks. Some cocktail historians say the **DAIQUIRI** is the first cocktail ever created. The story goes that Admiral Nelson of the Royal Navy found himself on the high seas with his crew ailing with scurvy, a sickness brought on by a lack of Vitamin C. His solution: Add fresh lime juice to the daily ration of rum. To make it more palatable, the chief steward also added sugar. You'll need:

1½ ounces 10 Cane rum
1½ ounces fresh lime juice
½ ounce simple syrup (see page 16)
Lime wedge

Place a cocktail glass in the freezer. Combine all the ingredients in a cocktail shaker; add ice and shake vigorously. Strain into the chilled glass, and add a lime wedge as a garnish.

Mama Was Right: Manners Matter

We hear it all the time: "What's *wrong* with that guy?" It's one of the most common refrains through the evening, whether a woman customer is reacting to a guy not paying for her drink, or chewing his gum too loudly, or watching the TV screen instead of looking at her.

We're not about to totally disagree with you. As guys who like to think of ourselves as chivalrous, we wish there were more men out there who still remembered to open doors and pick up the tab. But just because a man doesn't know how to act doesn't mean you won't feel better about yourself if *you* act with grace.

And here's another thing: Just because a man isn't necessarily conditioned to have good manners himself doesn't mean he's clueless about what good manners are.

Manners are in place to make other people feel comfortable and respected. And you always want to make any man you're interested in feel both of these things, at least if you want him to express interest back. More important, you want to end a night knowing that you did everything right. No matter what some guy did, or didn't, do.

We've seen so many men get turned off by the smallest things, because in their minds, if you're not on your best behavior the first time they meet you, they can only imagine how far south it goes after that. Remember, unlike women, men do not often imagine women as something other than what they appear to be at that moment. They take you as you are, and don't get into that possibility bullshit that you do—"Oh yeah, he's got the potential to do this or that if he just had my help." No man thinks, "Well, if I just had a conversation with her about the way she does so-and-so . . ." It ain't ever, ever gonna happen.

The good news is that what men expect and like is

very straightforward and easy to accomplish: Say please. Say thank you. And be aware of the people around you, and aware of yourself.

We are not saying you should be stiff or rigid. In fact, having a good hold on what is appropriate and alluring versus what isn't should make you more relaxed! And since a bar is all about fun, we want you relaxed. But if you can just make sure you have a few basics under your belt, you'll be more comfortable, you'll make the people around you more comfortable, and you're likely to attract a higher quality of man who doesn't consider doing shots of Jägermeister to be an appropriate Valentine's Day activity. No matter what, following these dos and don'ts is sure to win you the heart of the bartender, and who knows? Maybe even a free drink, if you're really good . . .

Use Your Inside Voice

We've seen women who think the way to attract a man's attention is to literally shriek with laughter, or to bray a story really loudly. "I get overwhelmed when a person I've just met seems to take over the room by yelling," says one customer. Adds another, "A lot of times, women confuse acting charismatic with being boisterous, and they're definitely not the same thing."

Trust us, if a man is going to notice you and be enticed by you, it's not because his ears are ringing. Also, a really loud voice in a bar can be a sign to men that you're easy prey. For whatever reason, men associate voices or laughs that are too loud with a kind of desperation. Dial it back a notch or two if you're worried about it. You can't go wrong speaking on the quiet side—it's always easy enough to speak up if the guy can't hear you well enough.

Ask Questions, But Nothing Too Personal

We've noticed that when women get nervous, sometimes they'll engage with men as if they were talking to their best girlfriends. Not a good idea. When we were telling this to one of our women friends, she said, "But I'm only trying to get him to talk about the things that matter to him!" It's a good intention, for sure. But you might want to watch how men interact with each other as a clue to gauge their comfort level; most buddies talk about the score of a game, not about their existential crises.

Ask a guy about his biggest heartache or if his mother drives him crazy sometimes, and chances are pretty good you'll be standing alone so fast you'll wonder if you were just talking to Snuffleupagus. To men, asking questions like that isn't creating intimacy, it's prying. And prying—yuck. It's rude and it's a turnoff. Instead, try asking about the best vacation he's ever had, or where he'd love to go if he won the lottery. By keeping it slightly *im*personal, you're allowing him to engage on whatever level makes him comfortable.

It can be a delicate balance acting interested in a man but not making him feel like he's getting the third degree. One way to check yourself is to ask yourself if you are doing all the questioning and he isn't following up about you and your life. And if he *does* decide that this is the perfect time to divulge his deepest, darkest issues, and they aren't very interesting, count your blessings that you've realized he bores the shit out of you while you're still in a place you can escape with ease.

If You're Happy and You Know It, Show It! (No Clapping Necessary)

You don't need to dig through your closet and find your pom-poms from high school, but a little of that overt, rah-rah attitude couldn't hurt if you're talking to a guy you're interested in. We can't count the number of times we've seen people look so close to hooking up and then bam, it's over. When we ask what happened, he'll say she obviously wasn't interested, when she'll be telling us that she was just trying to act coy.

Sometimes acting coy can be as simple as you're trying to play by some stupid "rules" that a stranger made up, and the ramifications can play out beyond the bar. "This whole thing about she's not supposed to call me, or she's supposed to wait two days to call me back is such a turnoff," says one friend. "How am I to know she's read some self-help book and that's what she's been told will keep me interested? What registers for me is that she doesn't like me enough to bother calling me back sooner, rather than later." If you're enjoying a guy's company, it's really nice to let that show.

Allow Him to Change the Subject

Sometimes when people get anxious they can go deaf because their brains are racing too fast to really hear what someone is saying. If he's answering a question politely and then switches the subject or flips it back to you, don't follow up. Chances are he doesn't want to talk about it. Believe us, as you probably know too well already, men will go on and on about subjects that interest them. If he's more taciturn on certain subjects, let them go.

"But how am I supposed to learn about who he is?" one female friend asked us. Well, we'd propose that you aren't meant to learn who he "is" in a bar. You're meant to get a sense of him, enough of a feeling about him to know whether or not you might like to see him again. So try not to do too much analyzing of the poor dude. In fact, try to do none. Sure, maybe the guy you're talking to doesn't share your love of dogs because his mother ruined him for any kind of intimacy, even with animals. Maybe. But he sure as hell doesn't want to think about it—not while he's at a bar. You're here to have fun, girl, and so is he. Save that for the post-game wrapup with your friends.

Banter Back

Part of being well mannered is knowing how to keep the conversation lively. There's nothing better than a woman who can volley back when a man is being funny or clever (even if he's the only one who thinks he's funny or clever). The first thing most men want? To feel great in bed. The second thing? To feel funny. (Plus, in guys' minds, they aren't unrelated: Sex can be really scary—thus performance anxiety, helllooo.)

The good news in this is that a guy doesn't necessarily need you to be Tina Fey—he just wants you to be open and receptive to *his* humor. So when he says something funny, respond with a laugh and an enthusiastic comeback, even if it's just a "that's hilarious." And we bet even on your shyest day you can be more playful than that.

Remember, the Barroom Isn't the Boardroom

There are some things that even the most enlightened man can still be sexist about, as much as he'll never admit it to you. Actually, there's usually one thing, and it is this: At the beginning of the game that is flirtation, men and women do best when they stick to the rules set up thousands of years ago. Now, these roles obviously have evolved enormously, and we don't for a second question that women are as powerful as men in every important way. But what we would remind you is that while men and women should be equal in the work-place, you don't *want* to be the same in a romantic in-teraction. That's what makes it romantic, that each of you plays a different and interesting part in the game.

Allow a man to do what he is programmed to do, and that is to preen. To feel important. To puff up his chest and feel like it is his job to woo you, to win you. And nothing is going to shoot down that instinct faster than your responding to his conversation with tales about how much money you make, or how you kick butt at work, or how you breezed through college with nothing but straight As. "I think men just aren't inter-ested in smart women," says one female friend. "As soon as I tell them that I'm a high-powered attorney, I can watch them shut down."

Well, we've actually watched her in action enough times to see what's going wrong, and it's that she literally says, within ten minutes of meeting a guy, "I'm a high-powered attorney." She isn't letting him make his own judgments, allowing him to realize she is powerful and successful on her own. And immediately, he's feeling like there's some competition that's been started. That kind of comment makes a guy want to say, "Oh yeah? Well, I'm a high-powered..."

You should certainly be comfortable presenting yourself as strong and capable, but do watch that in the first interactions with a guy, you're not making him feel like he has to compete—or worse, that he couldn't possibly compete. This isn't a dynamic you would want to have with a friend, or anyone you cared about—it's certainly not something you want to communicate by accident with a stranger who doesn't know you better. Let him have his moment to feel good talking to you about who he is without making it into a game of one-upmanship. If the evening goes well, you'll have plenty of time to tell him about yourself in ways that will make it clear how successful you are.

Save Religion and Politics for Date Number Two

The old rule is never talk about politics or religion at a bar, and there's a reason for it.

Most people will have one of three reactions to your political beliefs and stances: They will be bored. They will be annoyed. Or they will agree. And really, if it's the last, who cares because there's not much more to say anyway, and if it's the first two, there won't be much more to say, either, because the dude will have walked away two minutes into your lecture on Supreme Court justices. Everyone feels entitled to have a personal opinion, and we back that fully. But that doesn't mean you should jump right into a conversation and start asserting your views. It can destroy an intimate situation and be intimidating.

Steer Away from Talking About Fashion . . .

If children are meant to be seen but not heard, what you wear is meant to be seen but not talked about. Unless you're relating a fantasy about removing it piece by piece, of course. You're likely to alienate a guy pretty fast if you start talking about your passion for shopping, or at least make him speed through as much of the flirtation as possible to get to what he's after. In our experience, there's almost *always* a more interesting subject a woman can talk about than clothing. (Obviously there's the random metrosexual or fashion designer who is legitimately interested, but best to let the guy initiate it.)

. . . or Exes

This is pretty much the worst of the deal breakers. It's rude, it's exclusive, and it's a downer. When we asked guys in the bar about turn-ons and turnoffs, those same guys who said a smile was the number one turn-on (and that would be all of them) said hearing about exes was the number one turn*off.* To sum it up quickly: It is safe to say that men assume you're not a virgin, as much as they might not like to admit it. You don't need to remind them. As one customer said the other day when we were standing around talking about it, "Any woman who mentions an ex-boyfriend to me more than once is on the outs immediately, I don't care who she is. Nobody, including me, likes to hear about the greatest love or the biggest bastard in someone's life on the first date. It means that she's not focused on me, and I think it's usually some kind of a veiled warning about what she expects." Or, as his friend put it a little more succinctly,

"We know you've been banged six ways to Sunday by your ex. The last thing we want to do is hear about him and it when we're trying to close the deal."

Keep It About *Them*

We'll keep reminding you: Men are the most insecure of all earthly creatures. Anything you do, short of telling them they're the world's most perfect people and then acting like you mean it, can set off their deepest worries and concerns. So while you think you're just saying, "You remind me of this guy I went to high school with"—and it was a guy you went to high school with whom you really liked—the guy's head immediately starts spinning wondering what you meant by that. (One of the only times, we assure you, that a guy is gonna bother to try to figure out what you meant by something.) Not to mention feeling that you're judging him. "If a woman starts comparing me to people she knows, that makes me feel that she's already made up her mind about me and what I'm saying," explains one friend. Not to mention the all too important fact that if you're comparing him to other guys while he's still on the bar stool, he can only imagine what you're going to do when you both get to bed. Chances are you won't make it that far.

Steer Clear of Stories About Your Demons, Real or Imagined

Without question, for all of us, life can be very tough. But that's what friends and boyfriends are for, not the guy at the bar who wants to believe, for the moment at least, that you are nothing but sunshine and roses. The hard-knock stories are appropriate on, say, date number four (or at least two dates after you have your conversation about politics and religion). They're not for casual conversation, and they sure as hell aren't good fodder for flirtation.

And speaking of fodder for casual conversation, unless you're a professional athlete or a gourmet cook, try to stay off subjects about how often you go to the gym or what you ate that day, no matter how obsessed you are. If you think it's boring to *do* forty minutes of cardio and count calories, imagine how boring it is to hear about it.

Don't Ask "What's Your Favorite . . . ?"

There's absolutely nothing wrong with the intent behind this question—you're trying to get a feel for a guy
and what he likes. The problem, though, is an obvious
one. Go ahead and try it on yourself. What happened?
You froze, right? And that's while you're asking the
question to yourself, by yourself. Something about the
wording makes it seems like an exam question. Not to
mention that most of us don't have a favorite, but
many things we like. Instead, try: "What was the last
restaurant you went to that you really liked?" or
"What was the last trip you took that you really liked?"
He's not going to feel judged if he mentions one that
wasn't actually his last.

Don't Be Catty

Sure, we know after all these years of standing behind a bar that women snipe at other women when
they're feeling insecure. But for a man, putting your
claws out and taking a swipe at someone else signals
one thing and one thing only: That you aren't very

nice. And if you aren't nice, why the hell would a guy want to be with you? "I was talking to this woman I thought was great," one customer told us, "and all of a sudden she switches the conversation to her best friend across the bar, and starts talking about how her friend's boyfriend has just dumped her, but she should have seen it coming because she was never willing to give him a blow job. I was pretty horrified. I mean, it was none of my business, and maybe she was trying to tell me that *she* would be willing, but I was pretty grossed out. Selling out a friend to a stranger—that's just low."

That's an extreme example, but remember, for most men it's all about them, at least at the beginning. And if in the first meeting you are already critical or unkind about people, he immediately wonders what it is you would say about him later on. Trust us, no man is gonna risk it. Not when there are four other women trying to catch his eye at the same time.

Don't Have a Cat
(or Don't Admit to It Right Away)

We're sorry to be the ones to break it to you, but this is something that men and women feel so differently about, that it's amazing to us men and women ever manage to get together in the first place. We know that women love their cats. But we also know that men feel about cats the way they feel about going to baby showers on Super Bowl Sunday. We mean across the board. It's incredible to us how many times men responded to our question about what turned them off with: "She talks about her cats." (Let's not even get into dressing up your cat.) And don't roll your eyes and think these are just the assholes—we mean this was, without fail, in the top three of turnoffs. One of the nicer guys added, "Maybe it's just that I'm allergic," but regardless, it's a no-no. We can't explain why, but please, please trust us. The first time a guy should know you have a cat is when he comes over to your apartment, and even then you should limit it to a quick introduction. If he wants to bond with it, he will.

Safe Ways to Save the Conversation

Making conversation with a guy can be hard regardless of the circumstances, but the difficulty level certainly rises when you're in a crowded bar filled with noise and distractions. We asked our guy customers to give us some no-brainer conversation topics that would get them interested, and *keep* them interested.

- "It's pretty safe to assume that guys love gadgets. If a woman was looking for a new computer or a new camera, asking my opinion would be cool."
- "I like to talk about music—hearing what other people like to listen to is a great way to learn about them without getting too personal, and I usually come away with a new band or CD I want to check out. A woman will always get my attention by telling me she's bored with what's on her iPod, and asking me if I have any suggestions."

- "Talking about what movies are out there, what she's seen and wants to see, is a good topic. Plus, if I like her, I know that I can call her and ask her to go see one of them!"

- "I like the old what-if-you-won-the-lottery question. You get to hear someone else's fantasies and tell them yours, without feeling like a loser because you haven't actually scaled Mount Kilimanjaro yet. It also gives you good information about each other in terms of what your goals are, without making it feel like a job interview."

- "Here's one that would keep me going for hours: 'If you didn't do what you do now, what would you do instead?' Most people don't like their jobs, that's a given. And I don't feel that my job—I'm a lawyer—defines who I am. But my *dream* job is to be an architect, something that I think says a lot about who I am and what interests me. That's a good way for a woman to find out what a guy's passion is, apart from the rat race."

Cocktail

An exciting blend of spirits, spices, and juices rightfully carries the name of one of the greatest exotic dancers and double agents of the twentieth century: **MATA HARI**. At our bar, the recipe calls for chai-infused sweet vermouth. You can substitute regular sweet vermouth to make a tasty version at home, although we've included the recipe for chai vermouth in case you'd like to try that, instead. For one drink, you'll need:

1 ounce Courvoisier VS cognac

¾ ounce Cinzano sweet vermouth (or chai vermouth*)

1 ounce pomegranate juice

½ ounce fresh lemon juice

½ ounce simple syrup (see page 16)

Chill a glass in the freezer. Combine all the ingredients in a cocktail shaker; add ice and shake vigorously. Strain into the chilled glass.

*Chai vermouth: Place 2 chai tea bags and 2 cups Cinzano sweet vermouth in an airtight jar. Store at room temperature for 24 hours. Pour the infused vermouth back into the bottle of Cinzano to dilute it.

Listen Up—to Yourself

We've talked about how important it is to listen when you're flirting. But learning how to listen is far more than a tool of seduction. It's about quieting yourself down long enough to be able to really start hearing the guy in front of you so you can make informed choices about what it is you want to do throughout the night.

People will tell you exactly who they are if you listen. Likewise, with all your chatter, you can be giving away far more than you know, so why not play it safe? If you're nervous about letting too much silence pass, practice with your friends and wait two beats after they say something to respond.

Learning to listen to a guy is crucial for two reasons. The first is that he'll give you really valuable information he isn't even aware he's handing over. But the second reason is far sexier: There are few things as underrated in terms of seduction than a woman who is a good listener. Who doesn't feel special when someone is making you feel interesting?

Recently, we heard about this great study a psychologist did where a man walked into a bar and interacted normally with a couple of people. Then another man came in and interacted with the same people but didn't open his mouth other than to ask a couple of questions. They not only rated the quieter guy as a great listener, but rated him as a great *conversationalist.*

Listening isn't just a polite or passive thing for you to employ. It's giving you power—enormous power. Because while you sit there listening to some guy tell you about himself, you're hearing things you need to know—before the fantasies kick in. What you learn in a first meeting is sometimes the most valuable insight you'll have into a person for several months, because they're telling you the basics about themselves.

By hearing him talk about his mother, or how much he hates his job, or loves his dog, you are gathering crucial information about this person that, when the martini haze wears off, you can integrate into anything else you might learn about him in the future. Few people understand that that heartbreaking moment, three or six months into a relationship, when you suddenly see someone for "who they are" can largely be avoided in the first meeting. Even in a crowded bar, even feeling slightly tipsy. Usually that person isn't any different than they were the first time you met them, short of life-altering experiences like being hit by a truck. Trust us: Most men are far too simple to dissemble. *In almost every instance we've seen, what's gone wrong isn't that the man "turns out" to be a pig, but that the woman misunderstood the guy, or pretended the guy was someone else until she was forced to confront the cold, hard facts.*

If anything, it becomes even more important to really learn to listen when you are in a bar. Because you're seriously at a disadvantage the more you drink. As much as you may feel like everything is going your way as the margarita works its magic, in fact, everything is working against you. We, the bartenders, are there to sell as many drinks as we can. And those drinks are undermining your decision-making skills. As you get numbed out from the alcohol, you can stop hearing things you really, really need to hear, even if you don't want to. So take a deep breath and let the dude talk. A couple of quick tricks to know you're keeping your ears open:

You're Taking What He Says at Face Value

It may sound like the opposite of what you're supposed to be doing, but trust us. Picking up a guy, or being picked up by a guy, isn't a poker game. From what we see from our vantage point behind the bar, people's faces tend to be pretty expressive and open when they're out drinking. That means that when a guy is telling you about himself, *believe him.* Not the bullshit about his big yacht or his summers in St. Tropez—in our experience, no guy who lives a life like this will talk about it immediately, and if he does, he's a pig, so skip him on all counts. But when he says he's not into relationships over your first drink, or he's never seen himself with a family, we'd bet big money that he's telling the truth. Sorry to break it to you, sister, but chances are really good *you are not going to be the exception.*

That doesn't mean you can't enjoy your fantasies—

sure, maybe he'll meet your adorable little goddaughter and feel like he can't go another second without breeding with you—but we're not being pessimistic when we tell you men don't change their stripes any more than zebras do. And there are some mighty fine men (not to mention zebras) out there, so tell yourself in that first meeting that this is who the guy is. Can you live with it? Do you *want* to?

Each Topic Flows Organically into the Next

One way to keep a check on whether you're listening versus interviewing is to do a brief recap in your head about how the conversation is going. Are you asking a question, and then following up with a totally random one? If it's feeling like twenty questions, slow it down a bit so the conversation can become a little more relaxed. You can also try taking a two-beat pause to see if he asks you the same question back, which is a good sign you're listening to and interested in each other.

Try to ask questions that don't just result in yes or no answers, if you can help it. Some good conversation starters include talking about music, or vacation spots.

How to Tip Appropriately

- $1 a drink is fine, but if you're running a tab, consider leaving 20 percent of the total, as you would if you were dining.

- Don't tell the bartender you'll "Get him later." What that means to him is "Get him *never*," and he'll be slower to come back to you when you want your next round.

- If a bartender finds you attractive, he may give you a free drink. You should still tip him, even if the house isn't charging you.

- Don't punish the bartender because you think the drinks are too expensive. He didn't set the price, and you've chosen to drink them!

- Please don't leave loose change on the bar as a tip. Round up in dollar increments.

If you really panic, "What are you doing this weekend?" is a great one, since it will tell you a lot about him (is he going to the football game? to the opera?) without scaring him with anything too intimate.

Now Watch

Listening is crucial. But it's just as important to engage your other senses—in this case, your sight. Sometimes, in a crowded and loud bar, it's the only perception you will have, so it's good to hone it as much as possible.

No one knows that more than a bartender. It's part of our jobs to suss out every single person who comes into our bar and orders a drink. We need to know, from the second we spot him, that this could be the guy who's going to pick a fight at the end of the night. Or this woman is going to get sloppy drunk as fast as possible and needs a hand out. Or that another person is just the kind of person we want in our bar, because he or she is cool, sophisticated, and keeps it together. Just as we're sizing people up in a glance, so you should be, too.

We're not saying you shouldn't give people a second chance in real life. While the rules you learn about being a good and smart bar-goer should all serve you in the world as well, there is an element to bar-going that should keep you on your toes a little bit. Given how little time you have with someone in a bar, and how many distractions there are, it's important you don't miss the little clues that can lead to a much bigger picture of the person you're talking to.

It doesn't take us long to begin projecting what we *wish* on someone, rather than seeing them as who they are, and recognizing who *we* are.

While you're watching a man, you want to get a read on yourself, and you want to be honest about it. Where is the attraction coming from? Is it sexual? Emotional? Do you like what he's doing, or what he's saying?

You certainly don't need us to tell you that if you see a guy who's just your type, you're going to be attracted to him. But it's amazing to us, after all our years on the job, how naive women can be when it comes to the most basic signs that should scream "get the hell away!" We're about to tell you how and when to excuse yourself with grace, but for now, all we're asking is that when you see a guy you're interested in, you spend a little bit of time watching him from a distance and getting a sense of how he acts.

Extra, Extra! What His Accessories Say About Him

Just as you give away certain character traits without necessarily saying or doing anything, so does the guy in front of you. Take a quick look at what he's carrying and see what you can learn!

A BlackBerry: He's important enough at work that the company needs to be able to reach him at a moment's notice. (That doesn't mean he should be checking it while he's talking to you!)

A briefcase: You're looking at an important executive ... or a big dork. (The outfit should match the bag, so if he's wearing a nice suit it's safe to assume the former.)

A backpack: This guy's more laid-back, probably with a job that is artistic or at least doesn't require formal dress. Or, he's coming from the gym.

A money clip: He's organized and elegant, but doesn't like the bulk of a wallet. He's also unsentimental—no pictures tucked away with his driver's license!

A phone headset in his ear: A deal breaker, as far as we're concerned. When you come into a bar, you're there to disconnect. Business should be done in the office—or at least outside the door.

A Treo or Palm Pilot: He's got cash, and he's probably got his act together. Plus, if he's always got his date and address book with him, he can't ever say he lost your number or forgot an appointment!

A pager: You're going to be sharing this guy with whoever so desperately needs him on the other end, whether he's a doctor on call at a hospital or a party-animal who can't bear to miss a single shout-out from his friends.

Cocktail

Speaking of paying attention, one cocktail that's been sorely neglected is the *true* **MARGARITA**, which has become all too often associated with that awful, high-fructose artificial margarita mix. A margarita made from scratch, with real lime juice, is truly a masterpiece. You'll need:

1½ ounces Sauza Gold tequila

¾ ounces Cointreau

1½ ounces fresh lime juice

½ ounce simple syrup (see page 16)

Chill a glass in the freezer—a cocktail glass if you like your margaritas straight up, or a tumbler if you like it over ice. Combine all the ingredients in a cocktail shaker and shake vigorously. Strain into the chilled glass.

To Err Is Human, to Flirt Divine

We're going to break it to you: No amount of success in other areas of your life is going to serve you as well, at a bar, as the ability to flirt. Because flirting well is just a polite way of saying, "Damn, you turn me on."

Sure, some women are naturally gifted at it, without question. They're the women who have something about their energy that people just want to be near. But the good news is, as the best flirts in the world can tell you, it's definitely a learnable skill! Not just learnable, but, as our female friends have told us, pretty damn fun to practice.

By now, you're in the perfect place to get going: You're sharing drinks, you've learned the basics about each other. Now, it's time to make it fun.

What It's All About

The grand masters of seduction cover the gamut of personalities, but they all make men feel great as men. It's about making them feel like you want to be with them. One of the best flirts we ever met was a woman who had absolutely no artifice, or none that we noticed. But everything she said seemed sincere about wanting to be close—every single look, every single movement, was intensely focused on her target. And that's what it comes down to: charming the ass off a guy.

So how do you do that, exactly? First, we asked some of our buddies to tell us what it was a woman could do to keep their attention. Actually, we asked them what engaged them while they were talking to women that made them want to continue the conversation. Amazingly enough, it almost always had *nothing* to do with a woman's breast or butt size, and almost always involved some little sexy thing a woman could communicate on her worst hair day. Because it was always about communicating attraction to the guy.

"Eye contact does it for me," says one pal. "Her eyes always tell me so much more about her and her interest in me than our conversation. Sexy eyes and knowing how to use them is a huge turn-on." Adds another, "I really like it when a woman makes me feel like there's no one she'd rather be with and nothing else she'd rather be doing at the moment. All guys want to feel adored. That's the real reason we go to topless bars—tits can be had anywhere, after all."

So how can you perfect the art of bar seduction? So glad you asked.

Back to Manners and Listening . . .

. . . Which brings us back to men and their insecurity. That means it's your job, if you should accept it, to make them feel good about themselves from the outset. One easy way to do that is to make them feel like you're hearing them; when you let a guy talk, he feels important. It's dumb, but hey, you're the one who wants to be with 'em. As you can see from the sampling above, almost all of our friends mentioned eye contact as one of the top things you could do to make a guy interested.

Be a Flirt, and a Flirt Only

A great flirt can be a woman who doesn't suggest that anything is going to happen beyond the fun of the moment, and then doesn't let it progress further than that. Remember, the chase is usually better than the catch from a man's point of view. "My favorite women to flirt with are the ones who don't confuse the flirting with the sex," says one of our male friends. "They make it clear they're just having fun. That doesn't mean that it won't necessarily go any further, at some point down the line, but she's having fun in the moment of the banter and the getting-to-know-each-other part, and giving us both time to figure out where we want to go from here."

The other reason it's good to learn how to flirt, and to learn how to enjoy it, is it can help keep your expectations in check. If you can really enjoy flirting with a guy but don't feel the need to push it into going home with each other, you'll improve your chances radically of having a nice night. Remember, men tend to say whatever is necessary to get into your pants. You should never assume that any sexual encounter that happens at a first meeting is going to lead to anything else. If you're comfortable stopping it at a flirt and a good-night, you might protect your own feelings a bit more.

Focus!

The key to flirting in a bar is to create intimacy in a space where you're actually surrounded by other people. Don't be distracted by what's going on around you—focus on the person in front of you. "A woman who acts uninterested *is* uninterested," one friend insists. "I'm not sticking around to find out whether she's just thinking about work, or has trouble making eye contact. Boom. On to the next."

You can't imagine how many men we talked to seconded his opinion, which is great because eye contact is so easy for you to make, and it seems to do the trick with almost everyone we talked to. "The most annoying thing a woman can do is *not* make eye contact," another friend says. "If she's interested she's interested enough to look at me while she's talking. No matter how cute she is, if she has wandering eyes or isn't secure enough to look me in the eyes, she's not gonna work out."

One really important caveat: Merely making eye contact is *not* the same thing as flirting, nor is it interpreted by the guy across the bar as a sure signal you're interested in him. A lot of women we know think they're acting like Salome because while they laugh it up with their friends, they're occasionally glancing up at some guy for a few seconds. At the end of the night, they're confused or hurt about why the "coy" act didn't get them the attention they wanted. Meanwhile, the poor guy just thought she was looking up at the clock behind his head, or past him to see how long the wait for the bathroom was. If you're using eye contact to *make* contact, then you need to hold your gaze and add a smile, so the man knows it's for him.

Be Creative!

There are three questions men hear 99 percent of the time, each time they start talking to a woman: 1. What do you do? 2. Where are you from? 3. Where do you live? It's so shallow, and they know it's mechanical. They're also insecure enough as men to worry that you're asking these questions not because they're standard and safe, but because you have an agenda: By learning what they do, you're asking how much they make; by asking where they're from, you're asking how much their parents made; and by asking them where they live . . . well, you get the idea. One friend remembers being totally into this woman, "And then she says, 'How much money do you make?' I don't make enough money for that to be a turn-on. Although I'm not sure any amount of money would make that a turn-on."

How about instead trying this? Make eye contact, raise your glass, and mouth "cheers!" Now *that's* hot. Ask them how their day was—everyone loves to talk about themselves. What also can work, because it's nonthreatening, is asking a guy what he's drinking. If you do it well, he'll offer you a sip, and then you're off and running. Also, consider asking him if he wants a sip of something delicious you're drinking. Then don't take the drink back (like you want to swap spit?). Instead, tell him to keep it and enjoy it, and then he'll be obligated to buy you one. And when you've gotten his attention, and you want to learn about him, to see if you have common interests, tell him something about yourself. "I grew up in . . . " and then fill in the blanks. "This is what I do . . ." He'll be delighted to hop in with "I grew up next door!" Or, "I'm in the same field!" But you'll make it about offering up who you are, rather than judging him for how he is.

Give a Compliment

Compliments are just plain nice. They make people feel good about themselves. And the more specific, the better. It means that you took enough time to notice someone and acknowledge him. Pick out something that makes him individual or unique, whether it's a tattoo, a beautiful tie, or something that is printed on his T-shirt. What you want to avoid is commenting on anything that is a status symbol, like a watch, since that will make him think you're just after status.

Remember Why Men Flirt

Understand your father was right, at least about one thing: Men have one-track minds. Men like to think of themselves as fairly developed; they have long-term relationships, they own a business, they're good citizens. Who cares? It all goes back to the reality that the first thought on every man's mind when he meets a woman is "Can I or can't I sleep with her?" while women more often ask the question, "Will I or won't I sleep with him?"

That's because nature knows what it's doing. Women are the keepers of sex, whereas men are the keepers of romance. That means we each want what the other has. Simple, you think? Women give men sex, men give women romance. But it doesn't work that way. As you no doubt have experienced, men don't hold up their end of the bargain as well as you do. Men have a much harder time with their emotions— they're trained from childhood to deny how they're feeling. Think about how often you hear parents telling little boys not to cry. No wonder it's so hard to communicate with each other. No wonder it's so easy just to have sex and split.

Give the Situation Plenty of Space

The other night, a woman was sitting at a table, in the middle of a conversation with her friend. We watched her notice a guy, give him a quick smile, and then go back to her conversation. That was thrilling for the man, because there was contact. Half an hour later, she stood up and it felt comfortable for the guy to move in, who was all the more excited because there had been thirty minutes of wondering. When he finally approached, she continued to work it perfectly, coming up close to ask questions but then pulling back for the answers so she didn't crowd his space. Also, every time she moved in close to ask a question, it was clear she wasn't going to kiss him, but it certainly got him thinking about it.

Pace Yourself

Take your time. Whatever else men say, they want you to go slowly. Negotiate your space—earn the right to come in more closely, just as you would want a guy to do with you. You don't want someone just grabbing your leg; you want him to woo you. Guys want you to do the same.

Smile, Smile, Smile

Assuming you mean it, of course. Have we said it enough? A smile, like eye contact, will get you far. As one friend says, "It's *all* about the smile. Tall or short, fat or thin, blond or brunette, all of the women in my life, from one-night stands to relationships, had good smiles. There's something so powerful about a smile, because it can disarm you, leaving you completely vulnerable at just the right minute. Hair can be dyed, bodies can change, but smiles cannot be faked. If she has a good laugh, too, then it's a wrap. I have dated girls of all shapes and sizes, colors and ethnicities, but they all had that amazing ability to look at me and with one smile, let me remember why I was with them all over again." We couldn't have said it better ourselves.

Flirt Icons

If you need a quick refresher course in seduction, all you need is an evening at home with your DVD player. These women, each in her own unique way, transformed flirtation into an art form:

Grace Kelly in *To Catch a Thief*

Eva Marie Saint in *North by Northwest*

Audrey Hepburn in *Breakfast at Tiffany's*

Jennifer Beals in *Flashdance*

Renée Zellweger in *Jerry Maguire*

Natalie Wood in *West Side Story*

Vanessa Redgrave in *Camelot*

Nicole Kidman in *Moulin Rouge*

Cher in *Moonstruck*

Catherine Zeta-Jones in *Zorro*

Julia Roberts in *Mystic Pizza*

Anne Bancroft in *The Graduate*

Kristin Scott Thomas in *The English Patient*

Cocktail

FRAISE SAUVAGE (pronounced *frez so-vahge*) is French for "wild strawberry," and the cocktail with that name is fresh and exciting. Eating strawberries and drinking champagne are considered two aphrodisiac rituals; this cocktail combines the two into a liquid form of flirtation. For one drink, you'll need:

Strawberry

1 ounce Plymouth gin

½ ounce fresh lemon juice

½ ounce simple syrup (see page 16)

Splash of champagne

Chill a cocktail or martini glass in the freezer. Muddle or mash the strawberry in a cocktail shaker. Add the gin, lemon juice, and syrup. Strain into the chilled glass, and add a splash of champagne.

Some Signs Point to Go!

You've learned to be present, to be honest, and to keep the fantasies on hold. But sometimes, the reality is less than rosy. Sometimes you want to get out of a situation that's not going to turn out well as quickly as possible. At best, you won't waste any more of your evening out on some guy who's a loser. At worst, you'll save yourself from an interaction that may frighten you.

Since we spend our lives always on the lookout for warning signs with men in our bar, we've gotten really good at sizing up some obvious tip-offs that should make you walk in the other direction as quickly as possible.

His Behavior Suddenly Shifts When He Drinks

That's Jekyll and Hyde behavior, and it's a good sign that he's a pretty angry guy. Fine. They exist. But one of the things that makes us worry about some of our female customers is that they not only aren't dissuaded when a guy acts like a spook around them, but that they seem to almost glom on even more. *Hello?* You are not going to fix them!

We used to work at a place where this one celebrity would come in several times a week. Now, this guy was famous, and handsome, but he was a mean, mean drunk. Every night began the same way: a new woman by his side and a stiff vodka in front of him. And every night ended the same way: the woman walking away in tears. But it was the middle part that was always so sad. The more the guy drank, the more the woman realized that he was getting pretty angry—he usually bunched his fists, and we saw him raise them a couple of times at his dates, as well. But instead of walking away, the woman always, and we mean *always*, went into comfort mode. Putting her hand on his hand. Stroking his leg. Whispering calmly.

Remember how we said chances are good you're

not the exception? It's even truer in a situation where an abusive drunk is concerned. And really, is it worth finding out that you are an exception? The end of the story with this guy, by the way, is that he finally did punch a date in front of us, which was all we needed to tell him to get out and never come back. And let's just say we didn't just "tell" him, and we didn't do it nicely. You shouldn't have to wait for that to happen. Ever.

He's with a Pack of Friends

Obviously, there are exceptions to every situation, but this is one that can lead to trouble. A guy with a large group of other guys can start to fall into some very primitive behavior, especially once alcohol gets added to the mix. Men who are in a pack start to fall into pack behavior, which sets off the fight for who is going to be the alpha male, or the leader. Think about it: If he's talking to you, do you think he's trying to impress you, or is he trying to impress the group watching his progress? And if this is true, what do you think the goal of the group is? Do you honestly think he's going to impress them by saying he had a good "conversation"?

His Facial Muscles Get Tight

This happens to the guy who is a bully, just like the guy we were talking about before, but he has a little bit more of a handle on it. A little bit. This is the guy, as far as we're concerned, who is the most dangerous. The guy who raises his fist is being threatening in such an overt way it's impossible to miss. But the quiet bully is the one who can make you think, "Is it just me or is he a little out there?" This is the bar-goer whose face doesn't fit the conversation. He might be smiling, but it looks like he's gritting his teeth. Or he's smiling but his eyes aren't. Even if you fail to pick up on this right away, his expression is almost always followed by verbal cues that will make you more aware of what to look for the next time you see a guy who looks like he's had a sucky face lift.

The quiet bully is a definite type around bars, and an encounter with him plays out something like this: He wants to do something that you don't want to do, or tells a joke that you don't think is funny. This is the guy who says things like, "Well, you're clearly no fun tonight" or "What the hell is wrong with you?"

Now it's our turn to ask you a question—what the

SOME SIGNS POINT TO GO!

hell do you care what this guy thinks of you? Even if he's right and you're *not* that much fun tonight, our bet is you're pretty cool and he's being an asshole. No matter what, get away from him. Any interaction with a man, from meeting him in a bar to going out to dinner ten years into a relationship, is supposed to be about fun and nourishment. Being belittled didn't fit into either of these categories the last time we checked. Never stick around if you're feeling uncomfortable or pressured in any way. It's amazing to us how many women forget that a night out at a bar is supposed to be fun. And this isn't high school where the cool kids can torture you for the next year if you don't go along with their latest, greatest plan. If you're not having a good time, see ya!

He Orders Champagne

The last thing you thought you'd hear from us as a criticism, right? Sure, we love the champagne-ordering customer—all we have to do is open the bottle and we've made a mint. But we'd always prefer our female friends to date someone who doesn't, on the first meeting, tell the bartender to bring over a bottle of bubbly.

Our Pet-Peeve List of Drinks

1. **Mojitos in December**: Crushed mint, lime juice, and rum is a concoction meant for a warm summer day. And selfishly, we'd love not to have to spend the time it takes to crush those little mint leaves . . .

2. **Rum and Diet Coke**: If you're dieting, why are you drinking alcohol at all?

3. **Sour Apple martinis**: Drinks like these, which are artificially flavored, signal to us that you're not interested in the taste of the actual alcohol, which is, after all, our passion!

4. **Vodka and Red Bull**: One brings you down, one lifts you up, leaving you right where you started, with a hangover to boot. More important, the flavors simply don't go together. Drink a cocktail, or a soda.

5. **Extra dirty martinis**: This is essentially a glass of olive juice with a splash of vodka or gin in it, which takes away from the elegance of the alcohol and the drink itself.

That's because the guy can often be using it as a move to distract you from more important things (if he wasn't, wouldn't a glass of champagne for each of you do? He can always order another). You want to be impressed by what the man is telling you, but also by how he's treating the people around you. Dropping a huge amount of cash is fine, but a guy should never be distracting you from the quieter, subtler things you should be paying attention to.

He Orders Shots

Sure, we're biased, but we can pretty much tell you what a guy is going to be like as a date, even if just as a first date, from what he orders in a bar. Believe us, if you see it, night after night, you get the hang of it. And without exception, the guy who's ordering shots, unless he's already your friend, is the one to stay away from. There's only one reason he's choosing to drink like that, and that's because he wants to get fucked up.

He Sits and Never Makes a Move

We used to have a customer who still makes us shake our heads when we think about him. That's because in our minds, he was in some ways scarier than the guys who would act aggressive enough with women that they would scare some of them away. We used to call this guy the silent predator. He would come in every week and take a seat at the bar. He'd order his drink, and then he'd look around the room, finding his mark. But this guy was so clever he wouldn't actually look around—he'd look in the mirror, so no one could tell, and keep looking until he'd found the woman for him.

Because he was handsome, and because he was well mannered, and more important, because he was quiet, he had a way of getting that woman to come over to him every single time. He never left his bar seat. He'd just look in the mirror at his mark and let his gaze linger just a second too long, and bingo! In a few minutes, she'd be over there, "impressed" that he was confident enough to sit by himself, and assuming that there was nothing predatory about him, since he seemed to be doing anything *but* cruising the room. What almost every single woman missed was that this guy was, like so many other guys, after one thing and one thing only: getting another notch on his belt. And just being smooth about it doesn't make it not the case.

His Bar Manners Suck

Hey, we're not you, but let us tell you that if we were, we'd have two deal breakers. 1. He doesn't ask you what you'd like to drink. 2. He doesn't pay. As far as we're concerned, we don't care how far women's lib has come, or how much more money you're making, or how much people have forgotten their manners. Certain things about bars never change, which is probably why, like great white sharks, they survive no matter what. If you're talking to a guy, whether he's come up to you or you've come up to him, he should be watching for when you need a drink and ponying up the cash to pay for it. Period, end of story.

Speaking of those drinks, it's crucial—*crucial*—to know your limits. Because that voice that tells you to get out, to move on, only dulls with each cocktail you have. But no matter how much you've had to drink, if you're feeling endangered in any way, you should just leave without doing more than excusing yourself to go to the bathroom and finding the first exit, or talking to the bartender and giving him a heads-up.

He Says Anything Resembling "I Don't Play Games"

We can't say this enough. Because we all *do* play games when we're interacting with the other sex. But the guy who says he doesn't, in so many words, is trouble. Because what he's doing is setting himself an escape route. For instance, once he's said this to you, if he gets bored or tired of the relationship he can simply not return calls or cut off all communication. When you tell him that you don't know why he isn't responding anymore, he can simply say, "Why are you acting so neurotic? I told you I don't play games." And right there, not only has he broken any sense of trust or intimacy, he will make you feel that it was all your doing, because that's what *he* believes. It's not a position you want to put yourself in, because you'll find yourself feeling hurt and victimized, even if you didn't like him that much in the first place.

He's Rude to the Staff

And we don't say that just because we're bartenders. We say that because any man who doesn't show respect to strangers certainly isn't going to show it to the people he cares about. That's the kind of guy who thinks intimacy is an excuse to be an asshole. He should treat the people who are serving him as he would treat someone doing him a favor.

A Good Man Isn't That Hard to Find

Just as men can make themselves repellent in a bar setting, they can also act in ways that we think makes them worth getting to know. Or at least talking to! Here are some of the more subtle gestures we find impressive:

- He offers his bar stool to a woman, even if he isn't trying to pick her up.
- He pays for a woman's drink, even if he isn't trying to pick her up—signaled gracefully by replying to her thanking him with a simple "My pleasure," and then turning back to his conversation while he allows her to do the same.
- He begins his drink request with a "May I please?" rather than "Can I get?" Believe us, it may seem like a small thing, but it signals manners and respect that extend far beyond the way he treats the bartender.
- He signals for his friends to quiet down when they're being too loud.

- He's dressed appropriately for the setting, but even if that means he's wearing worn-in jeans, he's always well groomed and clean. That's a sign to us he has respect for himself, which is the very foundation necessary to respect others.

Cocktail

To help offset men who may be less than fabulous, we offer a drink that is truly grand: the **GRAND-FASHIONED**. It's a perfect dessert cocktail in the wintertime, because it calls for blood oranges, which go into season in December. If you can't find blood oranges, regular ones will do. For one drink, you'll need:

Half a blood orange, unpeeled, cut into quarters

¾ ounce fresh lime juice

1 teaspoon sugar

3 dashes of Angostura bitters

2 ounces Grand Marnier

Muddle or crush the blood orange wedges with the lime juice, sugar, and bitters in a cocktail shaker. Add the Grand Marnier and ice and shake vigorously. Pour the contents into a rocks glass.

It's Never Bad to Call It a Night

There are a few situations where it's really important to know how to excuse yourself politely and
with grace. One is that you're not into the guy. The
other is that he's freaking you out—you want to be
able to get yourself out of that situation with as little
drama as possible so you don't play into whatever issues he may have. And the other equally important but
opposite situation is that you really *do* like a guy, but
for some reason you have to leave.

How to Excuse Yourself When You're Bored

If you aren't interested in the guy and don't want to see him again, that's fairly simple. Exactly as you extract yourself from a conversation at a cocktail party that's run its course, or wrap up talking to an acquaintance you've run into on the street, you smile politely when there's a break in the conversation and say, "It's been really nice to meet you, but if you'll excuse me, I think I'd better . . ." Insert whatever you'd like in there. If you're in a bar with friends, then you can use them as an excuse. "I'll always just smile at a guy and tell him that I'd better get back to my friends, since I've deserted them long enough!" advises one woman friend. "If they want to take that personally, they can, but I think it's also a nice way to disengage by making it about something *other* than them."

Another friend of ours is more to the point than that, and while it is the simplest way to go, it also calls for feeling very secure in social situations. When she's had enough of talking to someone, she doesn't bother to elaborate or lie. She simply says, "It's been lovely to meet you, but you'll have to excuse me now." To a guy, there's something kind of reassuring about this, as abrupt as it may seem to you, because he doesn't have to sit there and wonder if she was just giving him an excuse for leaving or she really wanted to leave. This friend takes the guessing game out of it, without ever hurting someone's feelings. As we said, it can be tricky to do at the outset, but in the long run takes less energy, is more honest, and lets the guy off the hook. Remember, you don't owe an explanation to this dude that goes into any greater detail than something that boils down to "Thanks and see ya!"

How to Excuse Yourself If You're Feeling Threatened

This one is as simple as it gets. Truly. Because you owe this person absolutely nothing. The only thing that matters is getting out of the situation as quickly as you can. The best thing we can suggest is that you excuse yourself and go up to a bartender so you can give him a heads-up that there's a creep in the room. It's really important for us to know. And then you should just keep on walking.

It's better not to be confrontational with someone

who is making you feel unsafe, because you never know what could set him off. You think you're being reasonable, but it's impossible to reason with someone who is insane, or having a rage attack. So tell him you are going to the bathroom, or tell him you are going to get a drink, or tell him you have to excuse yourself for a moment, and then *get the hell out.*

It's not a bad idea, if you generally go out with the same group of friends, to have some kind of established code so that you can signal to each other if you're concerned things are getting out of control and it's time to leave, and fast.

How to Excuse Yourself When You Wish You Didn't Have To!

Now, what about those times when you *are* interested in a guy, and you *legitimately* have to excuse yourself? This is another situation when being completely forthright will only serve to your advantage. Look the guy in the eye and say, "I have had such a lovely time talking to you, but unfortunately, I promised earlier that I would . . ." If you really have shown him how you are feeling, he should have a pretty clear sense that you've had a nice time. Then follow it up with "I'd really like to see you again," or "I'd love to keep talking about . . ." And "Let me give you my number." If the guy is interested in more than a one-night stand, and feels that he connected with you, he will absolutely give you a call. And if he doesn't, consider it a blessing that you didn't waste any more time with him and blow off whatever else it was you'd committed to! Instead, your take-away can be that you enjoyed talking to a new guy, and also honored your other responsibilities.

The Top Ten Worst "Excuse Me" Excuses

We asked the guys in our bar to throw out the lamest things women had ever told them before they fled. Not that you would even think about using one of them, of course!

1. "I just got my period."
2. "I forgot to feed my dog."
3. "I need to call my mother."
4. "My roommate is locked out."
5. "I need to go back to work."
6. "I'm meeting my personal trainer at five AM."
7. "I ate something bad for lunch."
8. "My boyfriend's waiting for me."
9. "I think I might like women."
10. "I have a migraine."

Cocktail

Sometimes leaving is bittersweet. So is the **NEW YORK SOUR**, a classy, eye-catching cocktail that's as difficult to be done with as a good date. For one drink, you'll need:

1½ ounces Wild Turkey rye whiskey

¾ ounce fresh lemon juice

¼ ounce fresh orange juice

¾ ounce simple syrup (see page 16)

1 egg white (optional)

½ ounce dry red wine

Orange twist

Maraschino cherry

Pour all of the ingredients except for the wine, twist, and cherry into a mixing glass. Add ice and shake vigorously. Pour the contents into a rocks glass. Then, using a spoon, ladle the red wine over the cocktail so it floats on top. Garnish with the orange twist and cherry.

A Man Can Say "No" Without Saying a Word

We cannot begin to tell you the number of times the same scenario plays out, time after time, night after night. We watch a woman having a great time with a guy. He's buying her drinks, they're hanging out and laughing, and then suddenly, it's all gone wrong. But the thing is, she doesn't know it. It's as if, in her mind, he's suddenly turned on her and she can never figure out why.

Usually, we just shake our heads, because it's almost always for the same reasons. It's not that she's gotten less attractive to him. If anything, and we're sorry to have to bring up the dogginess of men again, he's invested enough time and money in their drinks at this point that he's willing to forgive a lot in case it works out. It's usually that she's just said something, or done something, that makes him think it's worth cutting bait and cutting his losses. Read on if you dare, but try not to wince. Believe us, every woman we care about has committed one of these bar sins at least once in her life. (Except for the story we heard about a woman asking a guy to buy her friend a drink, as well, when he offered to buy her one. We hope she's the only woman who's ever done that.) But that aside, whatever mistakes you've made, you're probably in pretty good company. And if we have it our way, you won't be making those mistakes again. Here are the things you might be doing to make him look for the exit—and how to know he's doing it.

You Disconnect, on Purpose or Not

Obviously, if you don't want to talk to the guy anymore, or you're looking to get out of the bar in general, slowing down the conversation or pulling back a bit is natural.

But sometimes we've watched women who swear to us they were really into the guy seem to suggest they'd rather be home knitting. A lot of times it's because they get scared they're being too forward, so they tone it down a little bit to make the guy want more. But the thing is, guys aren't subtle. They don't see that they're supposed to mix the outgoing person you were ten minutes ago with the reserved person you've just become, and presto! They've seen the real you. Because while you think you're playing coy, you're actually just reading cold.

A friend of ours decided just the other night that he wasn't going to stick around to see if he could follow through with this one woman he'd been talking to all night because she continued to excuse herself, every fifteen minutes or so, to go outside and have a cigarette when they were in the middle of a conversation. Understand, this dude doesn't have a problem with women who smoke—or at least it's not a deal breaker. But since he doesn't have a nicotine addiction, he didn't understand that she wasn't just trying to make an excuse to take breaks because he was boring her. If you're really interested in a guy, see if you can stick around for slightly longer intervals. Or ask him if he'd like to come join you, if you do in fact need to get up every fifteen minutes for a break. Otherwise, don't be surprised if there's someone else on your bar stool when you return.

You Engage with Other People

A guy absolutely wants to know that you'll get along with his friends and his mother. Like, a couple of months from now. But all he cares about right now is that you get along with him.

When we were asking our friends and customers what could turn them off a woman, the same answer came up again and again: talking to other guys around them. As one pointed out, "Even if I understand in the back of my head that she's doing it to impress me that other guys think she's witty and sexy, all I can think is, 'Fine. Then let one of the other guys have her.'"

Obviously, this isn't to say that you shouldn't be polite and nice to the bartender (of course), or the guy's friends if he's out with them and introducing you. But you should monitor your tone so that he understands that the way you're acting with him is special and different from the way you act with men in general. Remember, for that moment, he wants to believe that he's the only one in the room for you.

You Kvetch

We beg you to remember the facts of life: Women bond by going out and talking about every detail of their lives. Men bond by going to a football game and talking about nothing. Do not confuse them, please!

Even three martinis in, men will eye the nearest exit if you start to talk about trouble in your life. You think you're sharing an intimate moment; he sees a long, pot-holed road ahead if he doesn't kick the taco stand and kick it fast. "As soon as a woman starts talking about what's going wrong in her life, I automatically lose interest," one friend says. "I'd like to hear about those things maybe on date four or five, when we're really getting into the nitty-gritty of knowing each other. But isn't she supposed to be trying to impress me when we first meet? I know I'm sure as hell trying to impress her, and I'd like the same treatment back."

You Act Like a Crazy Person

To avoid coming across like that woman who thinks she's being charismatic when she's merely speaking way too loud and annoying everyone around her, when in doubt, keep your little "eccentricities" in check.

Because while your dramatic emotional life may be just that, it can read to men as nuts. As one of our friends says elegantly, "Sexiness is balance. Nothing is a bigger turnoff to me than a woman who seems unstable. That's not exciting. That's exhausting, and boring." Another friend agrees. "I'm not saying I want a woman who is emotionless," he explains, "but falling apart constantly just gets tiresome. Eventually, all men see it as a pointless cry for attention, or a passive-aggressive play for leverage." And either one ain't good.

You Invite Your Friends Over for a Peek

This one's complicated because, again, men's insecurity can make some situations seem like lose-lose. On one hand, if you're out at a bar with your friends and you don't introduce him when they pass by on their way to the bathroom, that's rude. On the other hand, you don't want to take your attention off him, or make him *think* you are. If the friends come, many men will go. "I hate it when a woman calls her friends over to judge me," one guy told us. "We just met, and I want to date her, not her friends. Few men can make *one* woman happy for long. Making a whole group of women happy is impossible."

You Confuse Flirting with Fighting

Remember the part about playing nicely with others? Well, we're gonna circle back to that for a minute, because another thing we hear all the time is women deciding that picking a playful fight with a guy is a way of showing him she's interested. It's not. "It drives me totally nuts to watch a woman think that she's being witty when she's just being argumentative," moans one guy who's happily found his match. "I love a witty woman—my fiancée can talk circles around me when she gets going—but I hate a woman who picks arguments that are not enlightening or entertaining, just exhausting."

And we can't believe we actually have to say this, but our friends have asked us to, since we have the chance: No hitting. Not flirtatiously. Not playfully. Not for nothing. "That drives me crazy!" one guy says. "It's this automatic go-to for a lot of women, where they get overexcited with some hormonal rush or something and she punches me in the arm to make a point. No, no, no. I'm not a sparring partner."

You Overromanticize

We love that women are romantics. Our friends love dating women who are romantic. If anything, your romanticism only helps men to step up to the plate, and then feel really good about themselves for doing it.

But creating an intimacy—having the ability to make even a bar feel like the most romantic place a man has ever been—has absolutely *nothing* to do with romanticizing everything and everyone else. Again, a man wants to feel like he has the potential to be the only one for you, and you have the potential to be the only one for him, even if it's just in that moment.

So how do women so often blow it? Leaking more information than they ever should about their hopes and dreams by going on and on about other people (and usually people the guy doesn't know, and after this, won't ever bother to get to know). "It happened just the other night," one friend remembers. "I'm having this great time with this woman, and she starts up about how her cousin's life is just the most perfect life she can imagine. She and her perfect husband have this perfect home and this perfect kid and who the hell else knows because I stopped listening." Another friend says, "When a woman does this, she seems to think I'm too stupid to know that she's telling me what her agenda is. I get it. But why do I need to know this when we just met? It makes me feel like it's 'insert guy A' into some puzzle, rather than letting whatever might happen between us unfold."

You Speak in Future Tense

We're still stunned, this many years later, by how many women turn the topic, after an hour with a guy, toward the future. Let's be brutally honest for a minute: You may have had your trousseau picked out since you were seven, but no man grows up longing to be married. *Not one.* Sure, they all assume at some point they'll settle down, have a couple of kids and a nice house somewhere, but the thought hardly fills him with the excitement of, say, the Super Bowl. How many weddings have you been to where the groom gives a toast that says something to the effect of "Wow, she snagged me when I least expected it"? As one of our buddies attests, speaking for so many men, "The worst thing a woman could do when we first meet is turn to me and say, 'So, what do you think about love?'"

So let's say that unknowingly, you may have erred in one of these directions. It's not too late to save the night, because you can *still* get out with your dignity intact. And that means recognizing he's mustering up the energy to cut bait, and then, do it first. Some quick ways to tell he's eyeing the exit door and it's time to get ready, set, run!

His Eyes Are on Anything but You

The most obvious sign is that he's looking around the bar, rather than at you. Obviously, this isn't going to be the case at a sports bar, where you all are going for the purpose of watching something else. But if you see him looking at his watch, looking behind you—hell, if he's really desperate, looking at the door—that's a good time to start counting down to the "nice to meet you" speech.

He's Drinking Fast and Not Reordering

If he's two for every one you're having, he's a drunk.
But if he's trying to slog through his drink as quickly
as possible while you sip discreetly, he's trying to get
out. Trust us—we're trained to look at where people
are in their drinks. If a man is finishing his drink
ahead of you—way ahead of you—and not ordering
another one, even if it's just a Coke or glass of water,
he's just itching to move on. Since the pretense of
being in a bar is having a drink, all a guy needs to do is
get rid of the pretense to get rid of you.

He's Making Friends with the
Whole Neighborhood

Men, as we have clearly established, have a very, very
limited attention span. You should be more than
enough to hold it, if he's even remotely interested. If
the guy you're talking to is suddenly acting like Mr.
Rogers, engaging with all your neighbors, begin to
make your elegant exit. It's one thing to get into a playful argument and turn to your neighbors for their

opinion, but trying to draw several other people into the conversation is a way for the guy to break the one-on-one. (It's also a good trick for you to know, when you want to do the same thing.) If he's a good guy, he won't want to leave you standing alone, but if the people on either side of you are talking to you, he can leave you in good company. But he *will* be leaving.

He's Moving Back

You go forward, he goes back. Sure, that's the way a lot of relationships between men and women go once they're dating, but it's not a good sign for you when you're hanging out in a bar. If you touch his leg and he pulls it away, or you go in to whisper something in his ear and he leans back, he's probably not thinking you're the one he wants to be close to later that night. Or, you have bad breath. Which means he's still not thinking you're the one he wants to be close to later that night.

Mending Your Heartache

Like the ancient hangover cures, there's nothing more reliable than the top ten, time-tested heartache comforts:

1. Take to your bed and cry
2. Get some exercise
3. Tell your friends you're off solids, and ask them to bring you liquid, STAT (vodka and chicken broth are both effective)
4. Rent *An Affair to Remember*—at least you're not crippled
5. Read love poems by Rumi—your guy never loved you that much, anyway
6. Volunteer
7. Buy yourself a bouquet of daffodils
8. Concentrate on work—you can always do better in that arena
9. Count your blessings
10. Drink yourself silly

Cocktail

Also known as a brandy stinger, the **NEW YORK NIGHTCAP** is a wonderful last drink to order from the bar. When Humphrey Bogart signals for a "nightcap" in an old film, this is what he's asking for. For one drink, you'll need:

2 ounces cognac or brandy
¾ ounce white crème de menthe

Chill a cocktail or martini glass. Pour the ingredients into a cocktail shaker; add ice and shake vigorously. Pour into the chilled glass.

You Don't Need a Home Run to Win the Game

Maybe there is *one* thing you think about more than what you're going to wear. And that's if you're going to sleep with him. And if you do sleep with him—or you don't—what are the consequences?

This is the time of the night when a lot of women make bad decisions. And the bad decision isn't saying yes. It's saying yes if that isn't what you are 100 percent sure you want. You will never, ever regret not having gone home with a guy if at any point in the evening you are questioning your decision. Or, more important, if you told yourself at the beginning of the night, before you had your first cocktail, that you had a different intention. You should trust the sober you who made a decision at the beginning of the night, not the one who has been wooed, in a slightly tipsy state, and perhaps swayed.

There is never any harm that can come from ending a lovely evening with a guy, giving him a kiss, and if he doesn't ask for your number, offering to give him yours. But you must be comfortable that you are giving it to him to call or not to call; you should never give away your number only on the condition in your heart that he *does* call. Then you will have given away not just your number but your power, and you'll let someone else affect your ability to be happy with yourself.

But if, in your heart, you are positive that you want to continue on in the evening with this guy, and go home with him (or have him come home with you), we're going to tell you something that whether or not it surprises you is guaranteed to save you a lot of hours of obsessing in the future. Ready? From that guy's point of view, whether you decide to sleep with him or you decide not to sleep with him, if you are dealing with an adult guy who is comfortable with himself, *it doesn't matter.*

No matter what certain rule-playing fanatics would

have you believe, every piece of information that a man needs to have an impression of you has been made hours before you decide whether or not you're going to have sex with him. Which means that many men have decided within a few minutes of meeting you, assuming you don't screw things up horribly, whether or not they want to hang out with you more.

We understand that it's an integral part of society that women shouldn't be seen as "easy," but trust us: You communicate to men that you're "easy" hours before they do or don't get you to bed. As we've said earlier, it can be because you're wearing clothes that make you seem too available. Or your voice is too loud. Or your jokes are too raunchy. But at the end of the night, as you leave a bar with a man, it's more important than ever that you follow the one piece of advice that informs everything else we have told you: Be comfortable with yourself. Be comfortable with the decision you are making. Feel empowered and in charge, so that the next morning, when you wake up without him— or the next week, when you don't hear from him—you know in your heart you did what was right for you.

Should he turn out to be one of those guys who is freaked out by a woman doing what *she* wants, by not engaging in game playing, by getting the sexual satisfaction that *she* needs, chances are good you don't want to see him again anyway. "I have to admit that when a woman sleeps with me right away, a small part of me loses respect for her," one very honest friend admits. But we'd also like to point out that this "honest" friend has almost no women friends, and the longest relationship he's been in can be counted by weeks. He is not comfortable with women. He is not interested in having women in his life in an intimate way. He is interested in sex. And if you decide to sleep with someone like that because that's what you're after, too, and you allow for the possibility—the good possibility—that that is all it is, you have nothing to regret. Remember, *you have not thrown yourself on him.* If you are going to sleep with him, it is because he has offered it out there as a possibility, as something he wants. And if *he* changes his mind the next day, and he freaks out about the decisions he made, *that is not your problem.* You have taken responsibility for yourself and done as you pleased.

Remember, we are talking very specifically about a guy you have met in a bar. If you are having a different kind of flirtation and wooing from a man—if, say, he asks you out for lunch, and then on another day to a movie, and then perhaps out for dinner—you should take your cues from him. If he's asking you out for lunch first, he wants to get to know you before you commit to any kind of sexual interaction. But if you're meeting at a bar, the intrinsic understanding and rules of engagement are different. When we asked one of our male buddies about how he approaches a date with someone he's gotten to know versus how he approaches a bar hookup, he said, "To be totally honest, if I'm going out to a bar and meeting someone there, my intention is almost always to hook up. If I end up liking her afterward, that's just a bonus. But if you want to earn my respect first, then you are risking it."

You're out looking for company. So is he. And if you both find it, good for you. You both got what you wanted, and there are no victims. No one did anything "shameful" or anything to be embarrassed about that the other didn't, as well.

Two of our best customers are a married couple who come in for a martini every Friday night before they go out. They're devoted to each other, and have been together for almost a decade after meeting in a bar (yes, it does happen!). And if you ask them both the story of their romance, they'll start to laugh and say it wasn't exactly romantic from the start. They picked each other up, went home and slept together, and that was that.

Likewise, there are plenty of relationships—if not most relationships—that don't make it past the month mark. And it's not because the woman "held out." A man is either interested in you or he's not. But if he's invested several hours in getting to know you and not meeting someone else out that night, he's hoping he's going to get laid for his trouble. That doesn't mean he thinks you're great. At the same time, a man who thinks you're great isn't going to think you're less great because you stop him at a kiss goodnight. Or because you decide you really want to sleep with him without getting to know him better.

For better or worse, in our society these days there are no right answers in terms of sexual protocol and timing. Which is, no doubt, why it's such an endless subject of debate, and why women—to most men's minds—obsess about it.

The only mistake you can make is to assume that if you sleep with him that first night, he's going to stick around to have coffee in the morning, or call you afterward. But again, that's not because you slept with him. That's because he had already decided that he wasn't hanging around for more than sex, regardless of the consequences. Most men will do whatever they can to get laid. The way to avoid any heartbreak on this subject is to be clear with a man that you are only expecting or wanting a one-night stand. As far as we're concerned, if you decide to go home with a guy, everything's a one-night stand unless the guy proves otherwise.

There's a lot to be said for getting to know each other, for fostering the excitement, for keeping the mystery in a relationship. It's not that different from sex itself: It's almost always better if you take your time and let the excitement build. But that doesn't mean you're going to undo everything you put into the night, no matter what decision you make.

Would men like you to sleep with them at the end of the night? Damn straight. Men will always go there first—they're biologically driven toward it, and for the most part, they're much more comfortable being physical in bed than they are talking on a bar stool. But remember: A man's wanting to sleep with you isn't another way of expressing that he wants to be in a relationship, or that he wants to get married, or even that he really loves you. Especially if you've just met in a bar. What he is expressing is that he really wants to sleep with you. You make the choice about what to do about it, but be clear that the possibility of more—again, if this is happening at a bar—is very slim.

Once again, we can't emphasize enough that *you have the power*. You are in the driver's seat. And as long as you practice safe sex so that you don't expose yourself or your partner to any diseases, the only person who is going to judge you is yourself.

So why not get off your own back and do what you want? Wait, or go for it. But no matter what, make sure the end of the evening is at least as much fun as the beginning and the middle of it. And whether that means a kiss, a handshake, or a wild romp in the hay, it's your decision to be made as an informed, responsible, and joyful adult. Be in the moment. Honor yourself.

Because if you do all of these things, if you are able to succeed in being true to yourself, you will find your match. In fact, you'll find many of them.

Good Check-Ins Before You Check Out

1. Are you sticking to your intention for the night as you laid it out earlier in the evening?

2. Can you feel good about calling your best friend and saying yes, you did indeed go home with *that* guy, and giggling about it?

3. Are you already thinking about Googling him, rather than letting it naturally unfold?

4. Do you know you never feel good after a one-night stand? What will make this time different?

5. If you sleep with him and he doesn't call you tomorrow, will you still have a nice day?

6. Will you remember the next morning, when you start to panic that he isn't calling, that there was a time, only hours ago, that you didn't think you'd care? Will you remember there will be a time soon when you'll feel that way again?

7. Are you OK if he wants to leave the lights on?

8. Are you already thinking about calling in sick because it's so far past your bedtime?

9. Are you sure you can stand up to him if he hesitates about using a condom?

10. Are you as confident as you should be that you will never, ever regret *not* going home with him? Have you told a friend to remind you?

Cocktail

We've mentioned that sometimes we growl when we're asked to make **MOJITOS** because of the time they take when we're busy behind the bar trying to get to other customers, but now that you're home safely, you have all the time in the world! Plus, we never said we didn't love 'em. For one drink, you'll need:

2 sprigs of mint

1½ ounces 10 Cane rum

1 ounce fresh lime juice

½ ounce simple syrup (see page 16)

1 ounce club soda

Place the mint in the bottom of a tall highball glass. Gently tap the mint with a muddler or a wooden spoon. Add the rum, lime juice, and simple syrup. Fill with ice and shake briefly. Top off with club soda.

You Are the Mistress of the Bar and All You Survey

Cheers to you! Because no matter what has changed for you about your bar-going experience, you've already begun to think about how you can change the way you see and feel about yourself. How you can feel more positive about the person you already are. How you can stop beating yourself up that you aren't someone else. How you can feel in control of how you act in and interact with the world.

All that is needed to put your best foot forward is to place faith in yourself. To have enough confidence that you can allow silence in a conversation so you can listen. To feel secure that your instincts, when you watch how someone behaves, serve you well. To feel open enough to risk making a joke, or acting silly, or bantering back. To respect yourself enough to feel shy if that's what you're feeling instead, and know that that's OK, and everyone has nights like that. To know that no matter what you're feeling when you walk into the bar that night, there are doubtless many others in that room who feel exactly the same way you do, and not *one* person in there who hasn't felt that way at some point.

As we've told you, a bar is a microcosm of the world. And the wonderful thing about the universe is that we're all here together, going through everything together. We can help each other, support each other, offering kindness and compassion freely to each other while we recognize that there will be days at the end of which we will really need a drink to take the edge off. And others when we'll want to a drink to celebrate. No matter what, we will continue to gather in bars, to offer unspoken companionship during our lives.

We hope that you will continue to grow into the potential we see in every single woman who has ever walked over the threshold of our bar. But remember, while we can offer encouragement, the rest is up to

you. Only you can awaken yourself, only you can change your life. And you're going to do that by looking inward, by paying attention to yourself, and paying attention to others. It's this simple: When you are free, you are happy. And when you're happy, you no longer need anything from the bar. It's all inside of you. And if you are beginning to realize that, please raise a glass of champagne and toast yourself. We'd pour it for you, but we're no longer needed.

Perfect Digestifs to End Your Night

Sipping a beautiful spirit before you go to bed can be a wonderful way to wrap up the evening. Here are some of our favorite digestifs:

Grappa

Single malt scotch

A dessert wine, like Muscato d'Asti

Sambuca

Amaro

Cognac

Armagnac

Fernet-Branca

Calvados

Acknowledgments

A special thank-you to Rebecca Ascher-Walsh and Suzanne O'Neill. To my parents, Nick and Deirdre Kosmas, for all your support. Thank you to my wife, Carolyn Kosmas, for inspiration and devotion and just putting up with me. Thank you, Billy Gilroy, Igor Hadzismajlovic, Henry Lafargue, Akiva Elstein, and Jeremy Spector for helping create something special. To all who participated in our focus groups, thank you for your help. To the team at Atria Books and Maria Carvainis. Special thanks to Donna Bagdasarian, without whom none of this would have been possible.

—JK

I would first like to thank my friend and partner Jason Kosmas for all his dreams, wisdom, hard work, and dedication to making this drinking world a better place over all those years while we worked behind the stick together. And I thank:

Rebecca Ascher-Walsh for her dedication, patience, insight, passion, and knowledge without which this book wouldn't be what it is. Blessed is the man who has her heart. Our agent Donna Bagdasarian for her love, support, initiative, vision, and true friendship. Donna, we love you.

Maria Carvainis, and all the staff at Maria Carvainis Agency.

Our editor, Suzanne O'Neill, for her understanding, hard work, charm, and courage in putting up with the two of us.

All the great people at Atria Books.

Gilbert John Barretto, who inspired, guided, and taught me how to be alive.

Our partners at Employees Only—Igor Hadzismajlovic, William Gilroy, Henry Lafargue, Jeremy Spector, and Akiva Elstein for their support, love, compassion, and dedication. We are deeply honored to be your friends and a part of this gang of real men. Guys—you rock.

All our staff at Employees Only, who provided us with the opportunity to become better and more awake people.

My family, who with their unconditional love have implanted seeds in me to hopefully become a man one day.

Dale DeGroff, who inspired and taught us how to walk courageously on the path of the professional bartender and face the consequences of that decision.

Keith McNally and Ana Opitz for the inspiration, opportunities, and lessons without which we wouldn't be able to be where we are as both people and bartenders.

All the "matrix-building, brain-washing" marketing and PR agencies of the world who showed us how not to do things.

Finally, thanks to all the souls who we nurtured, accepted, and provided for over countless nights over the bar. Thank you for teaching us.

—DZ